English in Action

2

Barbara H. Foley

Elizabeth R. Neblett

THOMSON

HEINLE

Australia • Canada • Mexico • Singapore • Spain • United Kingdom • United States

English in Action 2
by Barbara H. Foley and Elizabeth R. Neblett

Acquisition Editor: *Sherrise Roehr*
Director of Development: *James W. Brown*
Associate Developmental Editor: *Sarah Barnicle*
Editorial Assistant: *Audra Longert*
Marketing Manager: *Eric Bredenberg*
Director, Global ESL Training &
   Development: *Evelyn Nelson*
Senior Production Editor: *Maryellen Killeen*
Senior Print Buyer: *Mary Beth Hennebury*
Project Managers: *Tünde A. Dewey*
   Anita Raducanu

Compositor: *Pre-Press Co., Inc.*
Text Printer/Binder: *Transcontinental*
Text Designer: *Sue Gerald*
Cover Designer: *Gina Petti/Rotunda Design House*
Photo Researcher: *Jill Engebretson*
Unit Opener Art: *Zita Asbaghi*
Illustrators: *Scott MacNeill; Ray Medici*
   Glen Giron, Roger Acaya, Ibarra
   Cristostomo, Leo Cultura of Raketshop
   Design Studio, Philippines

Printed in Canada
   3 4 5 6 7 8 9 10   05 04 03

For more information contact Heinle, 25 Thomson Place, Boston, Massachusetts 02210 USA, or you can visit our Internet site at http://www.heinle.com

For permission to use material from this text or product contact us:
Tel: 1-800-730-2214
Fax: 1-800-730-2215
Web: www.thomsonrights.com

Library of Congress Cataloging-in-Publication Data

Foley, Barbara H.
   English in action I / Barbara H. Foley, Elizabeth R. Neblett.
     p. cm.
   The new grammar in action. ©1998.
   ISBN 0-8384-2828-2
     1. English language—Textbooks for foreign speakers.
   2. English language—Grammar—Problems, exercises, etc. I. Neblett, Elizabeth R. II. Foley, Barbara H. New grammar in action. III. Title.

   PE1128 .F559 2002
   428.2'4—dc21   2002017281

International Division List

ASIA
Thomson Learning
5 Shenton Way
#01-01 UIC Building
Singapore 068808
Tel: 65-6410-1200
Fax: 65-6410-1208

AUSTRALIA / NEW ZEALAND
Nelson Thomson Learning
102 Dodds Street
South Melbourne
Victoria 3205
Australia
Tel: 61-(0)3-9685-4111
Fax: 61-(0)3-9685-4199

BRAZIL
Thomson Pioneira Ltda
Rua Traipú, 114-3° Andar
Perdizes
01235-000 - São Paulo - SP
Brasil
Tel: 55 11 3665-9900
Fax: 55 11 3665-9901

CANADA
Nelson Thomson Learning
1120 Birchmount Road
Scarborough,
Ontario M1K 5G4
Canada
Tel: 416-752-9448
Fax: 416-752-8102

JAPAN
Thomson Learning
Nihonjisyo Brooks Bldg. 3-F
1-4-1 Kudankita
Chiyoda-ku
Tokyo 102-0073
Japan
Tel: 81-3-3511-4390
Fax: 81-3-3511-4391

KOREA
Thomson Learning
Suite 301 Richemont Building
114-5 Sung San-Dong Mapo-ku
Seoul 121-250
Korea
Tel: 82-2-322-4926
Fax: 82-2-322-4927

LATIN AMERICA
Thomson Learning
Séneca 53
Colonia Polanco
11560 México D.F.
México
Tel: 52-55-5281-2906
Fax: 52-55-5281-2656

SPAIN / PORTUGAL
Paraninfo Thomson Learning
Calle Magallanes 25
28015 – Madrid
España
Tel: 34-(0)91-446-3350
Fax: 34-(0)91-445-6218

TAIWAN
Thomson Learning
12F, No. 10 Heng Yang Road
Taipei, Taiwan, R.O.C.
Tel: 886-2-2375-1118
Fax: 886-2-2375-1119

EUROPE / MIDDLE EAST/AFRICA
Thomson Learning
High Holborn House
50 / 51 Bedford Row
London WC1R 4LR
United Kingdom
Tel: 44-20-7067-2500
Fax: 44-20-7067-2600

 Acknowledgments

We would like to acknowledge the many individuals who helped, encouraged, and supported us during the writing and production of this series. In keeping with an open-ended format, we would like to offer a matching exercise. Please be advised, there is more than one correct "match" for each person. Thank you all!

Jim Brown	• for your creative eye for art and design.
Eric Bredenberg	• for your enthusiasm and support.
Sherrise Roehr	• for your support, patience, and humor while guiding this project.
Maryellen Killeen	• for your faith in the authors.
Audra Longert	• for your smiles and your stories.
Tünde A. Dewey	• for your encouragement, comments, and suggestions.
All the Heinle sales reps	• for putting up with us!
The students at Union County College	• for your understanding of the needs of teachers and programs.
The faculty and staff at UCC	• for your keeping us all on schedule.
Our families	• for your help with research.

The authors and publisher would like to thank the following reviewers and consultants:

Linda Boice
Elk Grove Unified School District, Sacramento, CA

Rocio Castiblanco
Seminole Community College, Sanford, FL

Jared Erfle
Antelope Valley High School, Lancaster, CA

Rob Kustusch
Triton Community College, River Grove, IL

Patricia Long
Old Marshall Adult School, Sacramento, CA

Kathleen Newton
New York City Board of Education, Bronx, NY

Alberto Panizo
Miami-Dade Community College, Miami, FL

Eric Rosenbaum
Bronx Community College, Bronx, NY

Michaela Safadi
South Gate Community, South Gate, CA

Armando Valdez
Huantes Learning and Leadership Development Center, San Antonio, TX

Contents

Contents

To the Teacher

Many years ago, I attended an ESL workshop in which the presenter asked a full audience, "How many of you read the **To the Teacher** at the front of the text?" Two participants raised their hands. Since that time, I have begged my publishers to release me from this responsibility, but have always been overruled.

As a teacher, you can form a clear first impression of this book. Flip through the pages. Will the format appeal to your students? Look carefully through the table of contents. Are most of the structures and contexts that your program has established included in the text? Thumb slowly through a few units. Will the activities and exercises, the support, the pace be appropriate for your students? If you wish, you can even read the rest of **To the Teacher** below.

English in Action is a four-level core language series for ESL/EFL students. It is a comprehensive revision and expansion of *The New Grammar in Action*. The popularity of the original edition delighted us, but we heard the same requests over and over: "Please include more readings and pronunciation," and "Could you add a workbook?" In planning the revision, our publisher threw budgetary concerns to the wind and decided to produce a four color, redesigned version. The revision also allowed us, the authors, an opportunity to refine the text. We are writers, but we are also teachers. We wrote a unit, then immediately tried it out in the classroom. Activities, tasks, and exercises were added, deleted, and changed in an on-going process. Students provided daily and honest feedback.

This second book is designed for students who have had some exposure to English, such as students who have taken a basic course, false beginners, and adults who have lived in the United States for a few years.

The units in Book 2 branch from introductions to school, home and neighborhood, to work, and to past activities and future plans. The contexts are everyday places and situations. The units build gradually, giving students the vocabulary, the grammar, and the expressions to talk about the situations and themselves. Students see, hear, and practice the language of everyday life in a great variety of exercises and activities. Because this is the second book and students are somewhat unsure of themselves,

there is ever-present support in the form of grammar notes, examples, vocabulary boxes, and so on. By the end of Book 2, students should feel comfortable talking, reading, and writing about their lives using basic English phrases and sentences.

Each unit will take between five and seven hours of classroom time. If you have less time, you may need to choose the exercises you feel are the most appropriate for your students. You can assign some of the activities for homework. For example, after previewing **Writing Our Stories,** students can write their own stories at home, instead of in class. The short descriptions that follow give you an idea of the sections in each unit.

Finally, the book comes with an audio component. You need the audio program! The listening activities in the units are motivating and interesting. They provide other voices than that of the teacher. We have encouraged our adult students to buy the book/audio package. They tell us that they listen to the audio at home and in the car.

Dictionary

Each unit opens with a one- or two-page illustrated **Dictionary.** Students are asked to listen and repeat each item. All teachers realize that one repetition of vocabulary words does not produce mastery. Ask students to sit in groups and study the words together. Stage spelling bees. Play word bingo. Look for the same items in the classroom or school environment. Students must also study the words at home.

Active Grammar

Three to six pages of structured exercises present and practice the grammar of the unit. This second book integrates the new vocabulary and the grammar throughout all the activities in the unit. At this level, students can be expected to learn the basic structures of English and to feel more comfortable using the language. As students progress through this section, they will find a variety of supportive features. Artwork and photos illustrate the context clearly. Answer boxes show the verbs or nouns to use in the answers. For many of the exercises, the entire class will be working together with your direction and explanations. Other exercises have a pairwork icon 👥 — students can try these with a partner. You can walk around the classroom, listening to students and answering their questions.

Pronunciation

Within the **Active Grammar** section is an exercise that focuses on pronunciation. These are specific pronunciation points that complement the grammar or vocabulary of the lesson, such as plural *s*, contractions, numbers, and syllables.

Working Together

For these one to two pages, students work in pairs or groups, trying out their new language with cooperative tasks, such as interviewing partners, writing conversations, or arranging a person's daily schedule. The Student to Student exercises are information gap activities in which the students look at different pages and share information about maps, jobs, menus, prices, and other contexts. Be prepared—students will make lots of mistakes during the practice. This exploration of the language is an important step in gaining comfort and fluency in English. If your students represent several different languages, group students with classmates who speak a language other than their own.

The Big Picture

This is our favorite section. It integrates listening, vocabulary, and structure. A large, lively picture shows a particular setting, such as a street scene, a job interview, or vacation plans. Students listen to a short story or conversation, and then answer questions about the story, fill in exercises, review structures, or write conversations.

Reading

The reading expands the context of the lesson. We did not manipulate a selection so that every sentence fits into the structure presented in the unit! There are new vocabulary words and structures. Teachers can help ESL readers learn that understanding the main idea is primary. They can then go back over the material to find the details that are interesting or relevant. If students can find the information they need, it is not necessary to master or look up every word.

Writing Our Stories

In this writing section, students first read a paragraph written by an ESL student or teacher. By using checklists or fill-in sentences, students are directed to brainstorm about their own schools, families, jobs, etc. Students then have an opportunity to write about themselves. Several teachers have told us about the creative ways they share student writing, including publishing student magazines, designing a class Web page, and displaying stories and photos taken by their students.

Practicing on Your Own

This is simple: It's a homework section. Some teachers ask students to do the exercises in class. Another suggestion for homework is the audio component. Ask students to listen to it three or four more times, reviewing the vocabulary and the exercises they did in class. Our students tell us that they often write the story from the Big Picture as a dictation activity.

Looking at . . .

This is a convenient place for forms, math problems, or interesting information we located about the topic as we were writing the units.

Grammar Summary

Some teachers wanted this summary at the beginning of the unit; others were pleased to see it at the end. Use this section if and when you wish. Some students like to see the grammar up front, having a clear map of the developing grammar. We have found, though, that many of our students at this beginning level are confused with a clump of grammar explanations at the beginning of a unit. There are small grammar charts as needed throughout the unit. The ending summary brings them together.

I am sure we will be revising the text again in three or four years. We will be gathering your input during that time. You can always e-mail us at www.heinle.com with your comments, complaints, and suggestions.

About the Authors

Liz and I both work at Union County College in Elizabeth, New Jersey. We teach at the Institute for Intensive English, a large English as a Second Language program. Students from over 70 different countries study in our classes. Between us, Liz and I have been teaching at the college for over 40 years! When Liz isn't writing, she spends her time traveling, taking pictures, and watching her favorite baseball team, the New York Mets. Liz took many of the pictures in the texts, for which our students eagerly posed. In the warm weather, I can't start my day without a 15- or 20-mile bicycle ride. My idea of a good time always involves the outdoors: hiking, kayaking, or simply working in my garden.

Barbara H. Foley
Elizabeth R. Neblett

Photo Credits

This page constitutes an extension of the copyright page. We have made every effort to trace the ownership of all copyrighted material and to secure permission from copyright holders. In the event of any question arising as to the use of any material, we will be pleased to make the necessary corrections in future printings. Thanks are due to the following authors, publishers, and agents for permission to use the material indicated.

All photos courtesy of Elizabeth R. Neblett with the following exceptions:

p. 4, top left: Jeff Greenberg/Photo Edit

p. 4, center left: Harry Sieplinga.HMS Images/The Image Bank

p. 4, bottom left: Bruce Ayres/Stone

p. 10, center left: AP Photo/Stuart Ramson

p. 10, bottom right: AP Photo/Lenny Ignelzi

p. 10, bottom left: AP Photo/Terry Ashe

p. 42: Michael S. Yamashita/CORBIS

p. 48: Bob Jacobson/Index Stock Imagery

p. 56, center right: Myrleen Cate/Index Stock Imagery

p. 56, bottom right: Michelle D. Bridwell/Photo Edit

p. 72: Reuters NewMedia Inc./CORBIS

p. 88: Steve Dunwell/Index Stock Imagery

p. 94: Stephen Frisch/Stock Boston Inc/PictureQuest

p. 95: Jeff Greenberg/Photo Edit

p. 104: Scott Barrow, Inc./SuperStock

p. 134: Sean Murphy/Stone

p. 148, top right: Robert Santos/Index Stock Imagery

p. 148, bottom right: FoodPix/Getty Images

p. 188, top left: REUTERS/Gary Hershorn/TimePix

p. 188, top right: Hulton Archive/Getty Images

p. 188, center left: AP Photo/Butch Belair

p. 188, center right: AFP/CORBIS

p. 191 and 192: Jeffry W. Myers/Stock Boston/PictureQuest

p. 196: Reuters NewMedia Inc./CORBIS

p. 207, center left: AFP/CORBIS

p. 207, center: REUTERS/Mike Blake/Time Pix

p. 207, center right: Reuters NewMedia Inc./CORBIS

p. 207, bottom left: AP Photo/Ric Francis

p. 207, bottom center: Damian Strohmeyer/IPN/AURORA

p. 207, bottom right: Reuters NewMedia Inc./CORBIS

p. 210: Duomo/CORBIS

p. 211: David Young-Wolff/Photo Edit

Nice to Meet You

Dictionary: People and Places

A. Listen and repeat.

A: Hello. My name is Carlos.

B: Hi, Carlos. I'm Esperanza. Nice to meet you.

A: Nice to meet you, too.

student

teacher

child

children

school

home

work

single

married

divorced

a widow / a widower

I

you

we

they

he

she

it

Active Grammar: Present Tense—Be

A. Listen to these students introduce themselves.

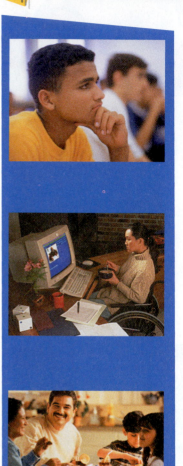

Hi. My name is Pablo. I am from Mexico.
I am 17 years old. I live in Texas.
I am a student at Adams High School.
I am at school now. I am in Room 9.

Hello. My name is So Jung. I am from Korea.
I am 24 years old. I am single.
I live in California.
I am a student at Edison Adult School.
I am at work now.

Good morning. My name is Diego.
I am from Honduras.
I am 37 years old. I am married.
I live in Virginia.
This is my wife, Ana.
We have two children. Junior is 8 years old, and
　 Melissa is 9.
I am a student at Lake Community College.
I am at home now.

B. Introduce yourself to the class.

My name is _____. I am from _____.

I am _____ years old.

I live in _____.

I am married. *or* I am single. *or* I am divorced.
　 or I am a widow / widower.

I have _____ children. *or* I don't have any children.

> When you meet someone for the first time, say *Nice to meet you.*

C. Pronouns. Say each sentence again, using *he, she, it,* or *they.*

> Pablo is at school. → He is at school.
> So Jung is at work. → She is at work.
> This school is large. → It is large.
> Adam and Anna are at home. → They are at home.

1. Pablo is from Mexico.
2. So Jung is from Korea.
3. Adam and Anna are married.
4. Pablo is single.
5. So Jung is at work.
6. Adam and Anna are at home.
7. This school is large.

8. The students are at school.
9. The teacher is in the classroom.
10. The book is on the desk.
11. The books are on the table.
12. The students are from India.
13. The door is open.
14. The teacher is at work.

 D. Pronunciation: Contractions. Listen and repeat.

> I am a student. → I'm a student.
> You are at school. → You're at school.
> He is single. → He's single.
> She is at home. → She's at home.
> It is the capital. → It's the capital.
> We are married. → We're married.
> They are at work. → They're at work.
> He is not from Cuba. → He isn't from Cuba.
> They are not here. → They aren't here.

 Say these sentences, using a contraction. Practice with a partner.

1. We are at school.
2. You are in the classroom.
3. They are in Room 5.
4. I am married.
5. He is at work.
6. She is a student.
7. I am in the classroom.

8. He is here.
9. She is from Mexico.
10. It is the capital of Texas.
11. She is not here today.
12. He is not at home.
13. They are not married.
14. They are not from China.

 *Yes/No Questions*

Keren and Kimberly are 18 years old. They're from Haiti.

A. Circle the correct answer.

1. Is Keren 18 years old?   Yes, she is.   No, she isn't.

2. Is Kimberly from Peru?   Yes, she is.   No, she isn't.

3. Are Keren and Kimberly twins?   Yes, they are.   No, they aren't.

4. Are they happy?   Yes, they are.   No, they aren't.

5. Are you 18 years old?   Yes, I am.   No, I'm not.

6. Are you a twin?   Yes, I am.   No, I'm not.

B. Answer.

1. Are you a student?

2. Are you at school now?

3. Are you married?

4. Is your teacher from the United States?

5. Is your teacher married?

6. Are the students from the United States?

7. Is your school large?

8. Is today Monday?

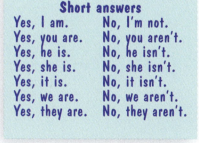

Short answers

Yes, I am.	No, I'm not.
Yes, you are.	No, you aren't.
Yes, he is.	No, he isn't.
Yes, she is.	No, she isn't.
Yes, it is.	No, it isn't.
Yes, we are.	No, we aren't.
Yes, they are.	No, they aren't.

C. Put the words in the questions in the correct order. Ask your partner the questions.

1. you / married / are / ? *Are you married?* _____

2. from / are / Japan / you / ? _____

3. school / this / in / Texas / is / ? _____

4. from / the teacher / is / California / ? _____

5. all the students / today / are / in class / ? _____

Completing a Registration Form

A. The alphabet. Listen and repeat.

Aa	Bb	Cc	Dd	Ee	Ff	Gg
Hh	Ii	Jj	Kk	Ll	Mm	Nn
Oo	Pp	Qq	Rr	Ss	Tt	Uu
Vv	Ww	Xx	Yy	Zz		

B. Numbers. Listen and repeat.

1	2	3	4	5	6	7	8	9	10
11	12	13	14	15	16	17	18	19	20
10	20	30	40	50	60	70	80	90	100

C. Listen and complete the registration form.

Please spell that.

SCHOOL REGISTRATION

NAME
_____

ADDRESS
Richmond   Virginia
CITY   STATE   ZIP CODE

_____
TELEPHONE NUMBER

_____
COUNTRY

D. Match the question and the answer.

1. What's your name?
2. What's your address?
3. And the city?
4. What's your zip code?
5. What's your phone number?
6. What country are you from?

a. It's 23223.
b. It's 555-7833.
c. I'm from Russia.
d. My name is Boris Galkin.
e. Richmond.
f. 514 North Avenue.

E. Complete with information about yourself.

```
SCHOOL REGISTRATION

_____
NAME

_____
ADDRESS

_____
CITY              STATE              ZIP CODE

_____
TELEPHONE NUMBER

_____
COUNTRY
```

F. Sit with a partner. Ask the questions in Exercise D. Complete the form with information about your partner.

```
SCHOOL REGISTRATION

_____
NAME

_____
ADDRESS

_____
CITY              STATE              ZIP CODE

_____
TELEPHONE NUMBER

_____
COUNTRY
```

Working Together: Student to Student

A. STUDENT A: Look below.
STUDENT B: Turn to page 10.

PART 1: Read these sentences to Student B.

1. She is married.
2. He isn't at work.
3. We are at school.
4. Boston is a city.
5. It isn't in Mexico.

6. She isn't from China.
7. I'm not a teacher.
8. He is 20 years old.
9. We are at school.
10. You are in class.

PART 2: Listen to Student B. Circle the verb form you hear.

11. He **is / isn't** a student.
12. She **is / isn't** at school.
13. We **are / aren't** from Russia.
14. **I'm / I'm not** married.
15. You **are / aren't** in Room 2.

16. They **are / aren't** at work.
17. She **is / isn't** single.
18. **I'm / I'm not** a student.
19. It **is / isn't** Monday.
20. They **are / aren't** from Japan.

Working Together: Student to Student

B. STUDENT B

PART 1: Listen to Student A. Circle the verb form you hear.

1. She **is / isn't** married.
2. He **is / isn't** at work.
3. We **are / aren't** at school.
4. Boston **is / isn't** a city.
5. It **is / isn't** in Mexico.
6. She **is / isn't** from China.
7. **I'm / I'm not** a teacher.
8. He **is / isn't** 20 years old.
9. We **are / aren't** at school.
10. You **are / aren't** in class.

PART 2: Read these sentences to Student A.

11. He is a student.
12. She isn't at school.
13. We aren't from Russia.
14. I'm not married.
15. You are in Room 2.
16. They aren't at work.
17. She is single.
18. I'm a student.
19. It isn't Monday.
20. They are from Japan.

C. People in the news.
Bring in pictures of people in the news: athletes, politicians, actors and actresses, singers, etc. In a group, talk about each person. Write three or four sentences about each person.

This is Gloria Estefan. She is a singer. She is married. She has two children. She is from Cuba.

This is Ichiro Suzuki. He is a baseball player. He's from Japan. He's on the Seattle Mariners team.

This is Hillary Clinton. She is a U.S. senator from New York. She is married. She has a daughter. Her name is Chelsea.

D. Class list. Introduce yourself to the class. Write your name on the chalkboard. Show your class the location of your native country on a world map.

Make a list of all the students in your class. Write their native countries.

Name	Country

 **A. Listen and complete the form.**

SCHOOL REGISTRATION

NAME
_____

ADDRESS
Kendall   **Florida**
_____
CITY   STATE   ZIP CODE

DATE OF BIRTH
_____

TELEPHONE NUMBER
_____

B. Put the words in the questions in the correct order. Then, write short answers.

1. at / is / work / Akiko / ?

   <u>Is Akiko at work?</u>_____   _____

2. Akiko / school / is / at / ?

   _____   _____

3. she / the office / is / in / ?

   _____   _____

4. in / she / is / her classroom / ?

   _____   _____

5. student / a / new / is / Akiko / ?

   _____   _____

6. Vietnam / she / is / from / ?

   _____   _____

C. Listen and write the questions.

1. <u>What's your name?</u>_____   My name is Akiko Tanaka.

2. _____   337 Bayard Avenue.

3. _____   555-4739.

4. _____   March 4, 1980.

5. _____   Japan.

D. Conversation. Practice this conversation with a partner. Write a new conversation with *your* names.

A: Are you a new student?

B: Yes, I am. My name is Akiko.

A: Hi, Akiko. My name is Marie.

B: Hi, Marie. Nice to meet you.

A: Nice to meet you, too. Welcome to our class.

Reading: My Teacher

A. Before You Read.

1. What is the name of your school?

2. What does ESL mean?

My name is Lynn Meng. I am a teacher at the Institute for Intensive English at Union County College. Union County College is in Elizabeth, New Jersey. Elizabeth is a big city. People from all over the world live in this city. We have a large English as a Second Language (ESL) program. More than 1,800 students are studying ESL. Our students are from 72 different countries and they speak 80 different languages. We have 70 teachers. I teach Level 3 and Level 5. The students are friendly and talkative. They study hard. I love my job!

My students like to ask me questions. Where are you from? Are you married? How old are you? I am from the United States. I live in New Jersey. I'm married and I have two daughters. One is in high school, and one is in college. My husband is from China. He is a librarian. Don't ask my age! I always say that I'm 25.

B. Complete this chart about Union County College and about your own school.

	Union County College	My School
Name of school	Union County College	
Number of students in the ESL program		
Number of countries		
Number of teachers		

Writing Our Stories: An Introduction

A. Read.

My name is Bibiana. I am from Slovakia. I am 27 years old. I am single. I am studying English at Union County College. I am in Level 5. I study three days a week, Monday, Wednesday, and Friday. On Monday and Wednesday, my class is from 8:00 to 10:30. My class is in room 403. My teacher is Lynn Meng.

B. Write about yourself.

My name is _____. I am from _____,
city

_____. I am _____ years old. I am _____.
country   married / single / divorced

I live in _____. I am studying English at _____.
state   school

I am in _____. I study _____ days a week:
class

_____. My class is in Room _____.
days

My teacher is _____.

Writing Note

The days of the week begin with capital letters: Sunday, Monday, Tuesday, Wednesday, Thursday, Friday, Saturday.

Practicing on Your Own

A. Pronouns. Rewrite these sentences, using *he, she, it,* or *they*.

1. Mary is a student.   She is a student. _____
2. Tom is at school. _____
3. Peter and John are students. _____
4. The teacher is here. _____
5. School is open. _____
6. Ana is single. _____
7. Lisa and Kate are at school. _____

B. Contractions. Rewrite these sentences, using a contraction.

1. I am a student.   I'm a student. _____
2. She is married. _____
3. It is Friday. _____
4. He is not at work. _____
5. It is hot today. _____
6. They are absent. _____
7. I am not a teacher. _____
8. She is not at school today. _____

C. *Be.* Complete these sentences, using *is, am,* or *are*.

1. He ____is____ at school.
2. They _____ at home.
3. I _____ in class.
4. She _____ on the bus.
5. We _____ students.
6. Jack _____ a student.
7. They _____ not from India.
8. They _____ married.
9. Marie _____ single.
10. Tom _____ friendly.
11. I _____ not from New York.
12. It _____ on the desk.
13. I _____ 20 years old.
14. It _____ Sunday.

Grammar Summary

▶ 1. Statements: *Be*

Affirmative

I	am	
We You They	are	at school.
He She It	is	

Negative

I	am not	
We You They	are not	at school.
He She It	is not	

▶ 2. Contractions

I am	→	I'**m**	I'**m** a student.
he is	→	he'**s**	He'**s** in my class.
she is	→	she'**s**	She'**s** from Mexico.
it is	→	it'**s**	It'**s** a big country.
you are	→	you'**re**	You'**re** at school.
they are	→	they'**re**	They'**re** from Vietnam.
we are	→	we'**re**	We'**re** students.
is not	→	**isn't**	She **isn't** here.
are not	→	**aren't**	They **aren't** here.

▶ 3. *Yes/No questions*

Questions	Short answers		
Am I a student?	Yes, you **are**.	No, you **aren't**.	No, you'**re not**.
Are you from Cuba?	Yes, I **am**.		No, I'**m not**.
Is he 16 years old?	Yes, he **is**.	No, he **isn't**.	No, he'**s not**.
Is she at work?	Yes, she **is**.	No, she **isn't**.	No, she'**s not**.
Are we at school?	Yes, you **are**.	No, you **aren't**.	No, you'**re not**.
Are you students?	Yes, we **are**.	No, we **aren't**.	No, we'**re not**.
Are they married?	Yes, they **are**.	No, they **aren't**.	No, they'**re not**.

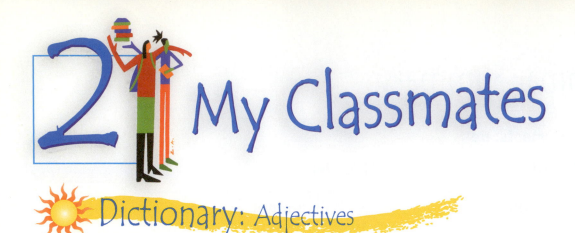

My Classmates

Dictionary: Adjectives

 A. Listen and repeat.

messy	neat	thirsty	hungry
beautiful	handsome	hardworking	lazy
talkative	quiet / shy	intelligent	tired

B. Describe each picture. Use an adjective from Exercise A.

1. ____thirsty____ 2. _____ 3. _____ 4. _____

5. _____ 6. _____ 7. _____ 8. _____

9. _____ 10. _____ 11. _____ 12. _____

C. Opposites. Write the opposite of each adjective. Use the words on the right.

1. clean   _____dirty_____

2. happy   _____

3. hot   _____

4. safe   _____

5. friendly   _____

6. nervous   _____

7. young   _____

8. noisy   _____

9. tall   _____

10. expensive   _____

11. easy   _____

12. heavy   _____

old
dangerous
quiet
cold
sad
unfriendly
✓dirty
cheap
thin
relaxed
difficult
short

D. Describe. Use an adjective to describe these people, places, and things.

1. The United States is _____.

2. My car is _____.

3. The students in this class are _____.

4. This classroom is _____.

5. The teacher is _____.

6. Canada is _____.

7. The street outside this building is _____.

8. English is _____.

E. Describe yourself. Choose four adjectives that describe *you!*

I'm _____, _____,

_____, and _____!

A. Complete the sentences, using adjectives.

1. Raisa is _neat_____.

2. She is _____.

3. She is _____, too.

4. She isn't _____.

5. Edward is _____.

6. He is _____.

7. He isn't _____.

8. Carmen is _____.

9. She is _____.

10. Juan is _____.

11. He is _____.

12. Carmen and Juan are _____.

13. They are _____.

14. They aren't _____.

B. _Who_ questions. Answer these questions about the pictures in Exercise A.

> Who is happy?
> Edward is.
> Juan and Carmen are.

1. Who is hardworking?

2. Who is messy?

3. Who is talkative?

4. Who is serious?

5. Who is neat?

6. Who is happy?

7. Who is short?

8. Who is tall?

9. Who is relaxed?

10. Who is young?

C. Answer these questions about your class.

| Yes, I am. | Yes, s/he is. | Yes, they are. | Yes, it is. |
| No, I'm not. | No, s/he isn't. | No, they aren't. | No, it isn't. |

1. Is your classroom hot?
2. Is your classroom cold?
3. Is your classroom large?
4. Is your book on your desk?
5. Is English difficult?
6. Are the students hardworking?
7. Are the students friendly?

8. Are the students relaxed?
9. Are the students intelligent?
10. Is your teacher tall?
11. Is your teacher tired?
12. Are you thirsty?
13. Are you friendly?
14. Are you talkative?

D. Write. Look at the pictures on page 20. Answer these questions.

1. Is Raisa at home?   _Yes, she is._
2. Is she messy?   _____
3. Is Edward talkative?   _____
4. Is he messy?   _____
5. Are Juan and Carmen in the park? _____
6. Are they happy?   _____
7. Are they nervous?   _____

E. Pronunciation: *Or* questions. Listen and repeat.

1. Is Raisa neat or messy?
2. Is Raisa lazy or hardworking?
3. Is Raisa at home or at work?
4. Is Edward relaxed or nervous?
5. Are Carmen and Juan at home or in the park?
6. Are they happy or sad?
7. Are they young or old?

> *Or* questions
> Is Raisa neat or messy?
> She's neat.

 Ask and answer the questions above with your partner.

 Countries and Cities

A. Continents. Where are these countries?

A: Where is <u>Korea</u> ?

B: It's in <u>Asia</u> .

Korea	Peru	Poland
Kenya	Egypt	Canada
Brazil	Vietnam	Turkey

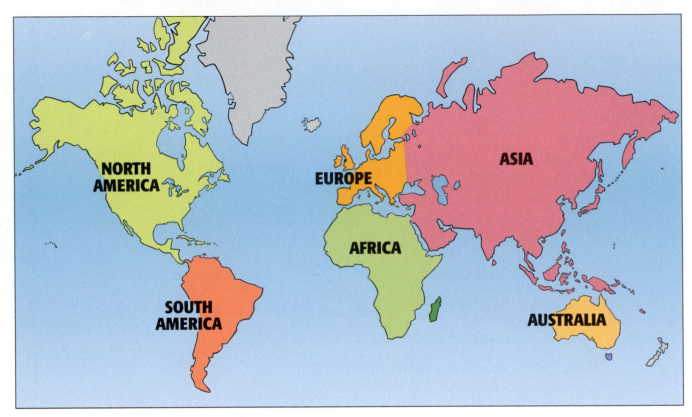

B. Capitals. What is the capital of each country? Unscramble the letters.

1. Spain   D M A D R I   <u>Madrid</u>

2. Russia   S M C O O W   _____

3. Portugal   B I L N S O   _____

4. Canada   T T A A W O   _____

5. Chile   A O I N G S A T   _____

6. France   S P R I A   _____

7. Japan   O O Y T K   _____

8. India   W E N L H I E D   _____

9. Thailand   G A K B O K N   _____

10. Ecuador   O T I U Q   _____

C. Match the questions to the correct answers.

1. What country are you from?   It's about 66 million.

2. Where is your country?   It's Cairo.

3. Is your country large or small?   It's in Africa.

4. What is the population?   I'm from Egypt.

5. What is the capital of your country?   It's large.

D. Sit with a partner. Write a conversation about your country. Practice the conversation.

A: What country are you from?   B: I'm from _____.

A: Where is your country?   B: It's in _____.

A: Is your country large or small? B: It's _____.

A: What is the population?   B: It's about _____.

A: What is the capital?   B: The capital is _____.

E. This city. Answer these questions about the city that your school is in. What do you like about this city? What don't you like?

1. What's the name of this city?

2. Is it large?

3. What's the population?

4. What state or province is this city in?

5. Is it the capital?

6. Is this city clean?

7. Is it safe in the daytime?

8. Is it safe at night?

9. Is this city busy?

10. Is this city quiet?

11. Is it hot today?

12. Are the people in this city friendly?

I like this city because _____.

I don't like this city because _____.

A. My classmates. Sit with a partner or in a small group. Use the adjectives here, and write about students in your class. Then, read a few of your sentences to the class.

Phoung is handsome.
Yelena and Diana are intelligent.

intelligent   talkative   tall

thin   tired

busy   young   hardworking

friendly   happy

B. Student to Student. Sit with another student. Ask your partner questions using these adjectives. Circle your partner's answer.

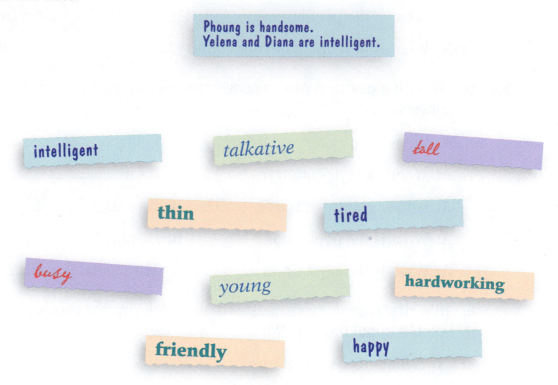

happy   sad

A: Are you happy or sad?
B: I'm happy.

happy   sad

1. happy   sad
2. relaxed   nervous
3. lazy   hardworking
4. shy   talkative
5. tall   short   medium height
6. old   young   middle aged

C. My country. Draw a simple map of your native country. Include the capital and the city or town you are from. Complete or circle the correct information.

I'm from _____ . It's a **large / small** country.

The capital of my country is _____ .

It's here, in the **north / south / east / west / center** of the country.

The capital of my country is **big / small.** It's **noisy / quiet.**

The population of my country is about _____ .

I'm from _____ . (name of town)

My country is **hot / cold / hot and cold.**

The people in my country are **friendly / unfriendly.**

Tell your group or your class about your native country. They can ask questions for more information.

A. Write three adjectives to describe Adam. Write three adjectives to describe Ben.

Adam   Ben

_____ friendly _____   _____

_____   _____

_____   _____

Ben   Adam

 B. Listen to the conversation between Adam and Ben. Then, listen to the questions and (circle) the correct answers.

1. **a.** in class   **b.** in the bookstore   **c.** in the cafeteria

2. **a.** a dictionary   **b.** an English book   **c.** a sandwich

3. **a.** Ben is.   **b.** Adam is.   **c.** Mr. Baxter is.

4. **a.** in room 312   **b.** at 9 o'clock   **c.** Mr. Baxter is.

5. **a.** Yes, he is.   **b.** No, he isn't.   **c.** Yes, they are.

6. **a.** Yes, he is.   **b.** He's from Poland.   **c.** He's from India.

7. **a.** to class   **b.** to the cafeteria   **c.** to the bookstore.

C. Write the answer.

Yes, he is.
No, he isn't.

1. Is Adam young? ___Yes, he is.___

2. Is Adam tall? _____

3. Is Adam talkative? _____

4. Is Adam hungry? _____

5. Is Ben heavy? _____

6. Is Ben friendly? _____

7. Is Ben a new student? _____

8. Is Ben happy? _____

D. Complete with *Who*, *Where*, *What*, or *What time*.

1. ___What___ country is Adam from?   He's from Poland.

2. _____ are Adam and Ben?   They're in the bookstore.

3. _____ is their class?   It's at nine o'clock.

4. _____ is from India?   Ben is.

5. _____ is their teacher?   Mr. Baxter is.

6. _____ are they going?   They're going to the cafeteria.

7. _____ is Ben buying?   He's buying a dictionary.

8. _____ is in the bookstore?   Ben and Adam are.

9. _____ is buying a dictionary?   Ben is.

10. _____ is their class?   It's in room 312.

E. Write a conversation. Sit with another student. Write a conversation between two students who are meeting for the first time.

A. Put an X on your home state on the map.

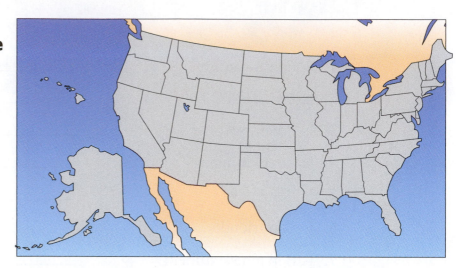

Where are these states?

California	New York
Texas	New Jersey
Arizona	Illinois
Florida	

The United States is a country of immigrants. The population of the United States is 280,000,000. Ten percent of the population was born in another country. That means that more than 28,000,000 people came to the United States as children or as adults. Most immigrants live in seven states: California, Arizona, Texas, Florida, New York, New Jersey, and Illinois. Why are these states so popular? First, many immigrants live in these states. New immigrants often come and stay with their families. Next, three of the states, California, Arizona, and Texas border on Mexico. Almost half of the immigrants to the United States are from Mexico and these states are near Mexico. Finally, these seven states have many large cities. There are many jobs for the new immigrants.

B. Circle Yes or No.

1. Many immigrants come to the United States.   Yes   No
2. There are 280,000,000 immigrants in the U.S.   Yes   No
3. Almost half of all immigrants are children.   Yes   No
4. Many immigrants have family here.   Yes   No
5. Most immigrants want jobs.   Yes   No
6. Large cities have many jobs.   Yes   No
7. Florida borders on Mexico.   Yes   No
8. Most immigrants are from Mexico.   Yes   No

C. Discuss. What state do you live in? Why did you choose to live in this state?

Writing Our Stories: My Country

A. Read.

I am from South Korea. Korea is a small country in Asia. There are many people in Korea. The population is about 46,000,000. I am from Seoul. Seoul is the capital. It is in the north, on the Han River. Seoul is a big, busy city. Korea is hot in the summer and cold in the winter. The people in my country are busy, happy, and friendly.

B. Write.

I am from _____. _____ is a _____
                                                          large/small

country in _____. The population is about _____.
              continent

I am from _____. _____

_____

_____

_____

_____

_____

_____

Writing Note

The names of cities, states, and countries begin with capital letters: Los Angeles, New York, Egypt.

Practicing on Your Own

A. Write the opposite of each adjective.

1. dry _____wet_____
2. neat _____
3. small _____
4. sad _____
5. new _____

6. hardworking _____
7. relaxed _____
8. old _____
9. friendly _____
10. expensive _____

B. My class. Put the words in each question in the correct order. Then, answer the questions.

1. you / are / tired / ?

   Are you tired? _____ _____

2. teacher / your / is / busy / ?

   _____ _____

3. is / class / large / your / ?

   _____ _____

4. friendly / are / students / the / ?

   _____ _____

5. your / teacher / relaxed / is / ?

   _____ _____

6. hungry / you / are / ?

   _____ _____

7. students / are / the / talkative / ?

   _____ _____

8. school / is / your / noisy / ?

   _____ _____

9. classroom / small / is / your / ?

   _____ _____

10. at / you / are / school / now / ?

   _____ _____

A. What is the population of each country?

3,000,000	three million
37,000,000	thirty-seven million
356,000,000	three hundred fifty-six million

Kenya	30,000,000	Egypt	66,000,000
Ukraine	51,000,000	The Philippines	73,000,000
Canada	31,000,000	Russia	148,000,000
Turkey	65,000,000	Brazil	166,000,000
Kazakhstan	17,000,000	Nigeria	107,000,000

Grammar Summary

1. Adjectives

   a. Adjectives describe a noun (a person, place, or thing).
   She's **tall.**

   b. Adjectives are the same for both singular and plural words.
   She's **young.**   They're **young.**

   c. Adjectives also come **before** a noun (a person, place, or thing).
   He's a **busy** student.

2. *Who* questions

Who is intelligent?	I am.
Who is talkative?	Hector is.
Who is at school?	The students are.

3. *Or* questions

Are you talkative **or** quiet?	I'm talkative.
Is Canada large **or** small?	It's large.
Are the windows clean **or** dirty?	They're clean.

3 At School

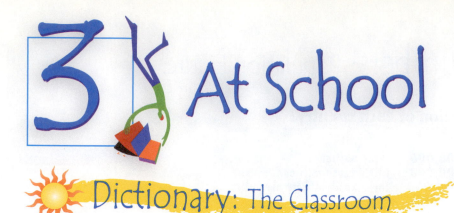

Dictionary: The Classroom

A. Listen and repeat.

backpack	computer	map	pencil	tape recorder
bookcase	desk	man	pencil sharpener	window
chair	dictionary	men	printer	woman
chalkboard	eraser	notebook	student	women
clock	examination	pen	table	

B. Label the people and the classroom objects.

People

_____　　_____　　_____

On the wall

　　　　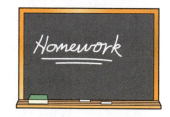

_____　　_____　　_____

Furniture

_____　　_____　　_____

Around the room

_____ _____ _____

On the desk

C. Look around your classroom. Write 10 more classroom objects. Your teacher may help you with the vocabulary and spelling.

1. _____
2. _____
3. _____
4. _____
5. _____

6. _____
7. _____
8. _____
9. _____
10. _____

Active Grammar: Singular and Plural Nouns

A. Singular nouns. Write *a* or *an*.

1. __a__ large bookcase

2. __an__ eraser

3. _____ expensive pen

4. _____ thin notebook

5. _____ excellent student

6. _____ U.S. map

7. _____ handsome man

8. _____ American teacher

9. _____ electronic dictionary

10. _____ young woman

11. _____ pink eraser

12. _____ English class

13. _____ big desk

14. _____ world map

15. _____ sharp pencil

16. _____ digital clock

17. _____ Asian student

B. Plural nouns. Write the plural of the nouns.

1. Add *s* to make a plural noun: erasers, pens, students
2. Add *es* to words that end in -s, -ch, -sh: watches
3. Change *y* to *i* and add *es:* cities
4. Do <u>not</u> add an *s* to adjectives: young students

1. a bookcase ____bookcases____

2. a printer _____

3. a computer _____

4. a dictionary _____

5. a teacher _____

6. a desk _____

7. a class _____

8. a man _____

9. a map _____

10. an exam _____

11. a woman _____

12. a notebook _____

man—men   woman—women   child—children

C. Pronunciation: Final s. Listen and (circle.)

1.	backpack	backpacks	10. table	tables
2.	bookcase	bookcases	11. class	classes
3.	clock	clocks	12. eraser	erasers
4.	teacher	teachers	13. man	men
5.	tape recorder	tape recorders	14. pencil	pencils
6.	woman	women	15. map	maps
7.	notebook	notebooks	16. dictionary	dictionaries
8.	student	students	17. desk	desks
9.	examination	examinations	18. computer	computers

 Practice reading the words with a partner.

D. Review. Look around your classroom. Write seven singular nouns and seven plural nouns. Add *a* or *an* to the singular nouns. Add *s* or *es* to the plural nouns.

Singular Nouns	**Plural Nouns**
a clock	windows
_____	_____
_____	_____
_____	_____
_____	_____
_____	_____
_____	_____

Telling Time

A. Listen and repeat.

3:00	three o'clock	3:05	three-oh five	3:30	three thirty
6:00	six o'clock	3:10	three ten	3:45	three forty-five
9:00	nine o'clock	3:15	three fifteen	3:50	three fifty
12:00	twelve o'clock	12:00 P.M. — noon		12:00 A.M. — midnight	

B. Read each clock. Write the correct time under each clock.

1. It's <u>six forty-five</u>.

2. It's _____.

3. It's _____.

4. It's _____.

 C. Listen and (circle).

1.	**a.**	(3:05)	**b.**	3:15	**c.**	3:50
2.	**a.**	4:15	**b.**	4:40	**c.**	4:45
3.	**a.**	12:00	**b.**	12:20	**c.**	12:30
4.	**a.**	1:05	**b.**	1:25	**c.**	1:55
5.	**a.**	2:10	**b.**	2:20	**c.**	2:30
6.	**a.**	10:15	**b.**	10:40	**c.**	10:50

D. Complete.

1. My English class begins at _____.

2. My English class ends at _____.

3. I work from _____ to _____.

> **around = approximately**
> **about = approximately**
> I get home at **about 7:00**.

Dictionary: Inside the School Building

A. Listen and repeat.

the auditorium	the director's office	the principal's office	the ground floor
the bookstore	the elevator	the restrooms	the first floor
the cafeteria	the gymnasium / the gym	the stairs	the second floor
the computer center	the library	the theater	the third floor
the counselor's office	the nurse's office	the tutoring center	the fourth floor

B. Label the places in the school.

1. _____

2. _____

3. _____

4. _____

5. _____

6. _____

7. _____

8. _____

9. _____

10. _____

11. _____

12. _____

C. Read and (circle) about your school.

1. My classroom is on the third floor.   Yes   No
2. There is an elevator in my school.   Yes   No
3. There is a gymnasium in my school.   Yes   No
4. There is a library in my school.   Yes   No
5. There are restrooms on the first floor.   Yes   No
6. There is a nurse's office in my school.   Yes   No
7. There are three floors in this building.   Yes   No
8. There is a bookstore on this floor.   Yes   No

 D. Pair practice. Ask and answer these questions with a partner.

Is there a cafeteria in the building?

Yes , there is.

Are there computers in this room?

No, there aren't.

Yes/No questions
Is there an elevator in the school?
No, there isn't.

Are there restrooms on this floor?
Yes, there are.

1.

2.

3.

4.

5.

6.

A. Look at the picture. With a group of students, write sentences about the picture. Use *There is / There are.*

1. _____
2. _____
3. _____
4. _____
5. _____
6. _____
7. _____
8. _____

B. The ideal classroom. With a group of students, design a classroom. What is in your classroom? On a sheet of paper, draw a picture of the classroom. Then, tell your classmates about your ideal classroom.

The Big Picture: My New Classroom

A. Vocabulary. Make a vocabulary list of the items in the classrooms below.

Old Classroom

New Classroom

B. Listen and look at the pictures.

C. Listen and circle.

1. old classroom   new classroom   5. old classroom   new classroom
2. old classroom   new classroom   6. old classroom   new classroom
3. old classroom   new classroom   7. old classroom   new classroom
4. old classroom   new classroom   8. old classroom   new classroom

D. Complete.

> There is old paint on the walls.   There is no teacher in the old room.
> There are two bookcases.   There are no students in the old room.

1. _There is_ _____ old paint on the walls in the old classroom.

2. _____ desks in the old classroom.

3. _____ a clock over the door in the old classroom.

4. _____ bookcases in the old classroom.

5. _____ a big bookcase in the new classroom.

6. _____ three tables in the new classroom.

7. _____ a world map in the new classroom.

8. _____ digital clock in the new classroom.

9. _____ a big window in the new classroom.

10. _____ windows in the old classroom.

E. Answer the questions about the new classroom.

1. Is there a window in the classroom?   _____
2. Are there three maps on the wall?   _____
3. Is there a bookcase in the classroom?   _____
4. Are there desks for the students?   _____
5. Is there a telephone in the classroom?   _____

Reading: A One-Room Schoolhouse

A. Before You Read.

1. Where is Minnesota?
2. How many rooms and classes are in your school?

Sometimes, there are only a small number of children in a community. For example, maybe there is only one child in the first grade, five children in the third grade, and three children in the sixth grade. Maybe there are no children in the fifth grade. In this situation, a regular-sized school is too big. In some small communities, there is a one-room schoolhouse, but this is very unusual.

There is a one-room schoolhouse in northern Minnesota, the Angle Inlet School. This school is near the border of Canada. In this school, there are students from kindergarten to sixth grade. In Spring 2000, there were fifteen students, seven girls, and eight boys. Some of the children live on islands. Some of the children live on the mainland of Minnesota, but there are no good roads for cars and buses. The students go to school by boat or by snowmobile in the wintertime.

Everything that the students need is in one big classroom. There is one teacher. There are only fifteen students. There are desks and chairs for the students. There is a big desk for the teacher. There is a U.S. map on the wall. For music lessons, there is a piano. There are three computers, so the students and the teacher can use the Internet. They can communicate with students in other schools. There is even a small library with five or six bookcases. This school is a small school, but the students are happy there.

B. Read and circle.

1.	There are one-room schoolhouses in big cities.	Yes	No
2.	The one-room schoolhouse is in Minnesota.	Yes	No
3.	There are three teachers for the class.	Yes	No
4.	There are many rooms in the school.	Yes	No
5.	The students go to school by bus.	Yes	No
6.	There are music lessons for the students.	Yes	No
7.	There are many computers in the classroom.	Yes	No

Writing Our Stories: My Classroom

A. Read.

This is our classroom. We're in Room 202. There are three men and twelve women in my class. Our classroom is small, but it is comfortable. Our teacher is Mrs. Mahoney. There is one computer for the teacher, and there is one computer lab on the third floor. There's a U.S. map on the wall. There are no bookcases, but there are desks for all the students.

There are two floors in our building. The building is small. There's a small library. There is no elevator, but we are comfortable here.

B. Check (✓) the objects in your classroom and building.

_____ a man	_____ men	_____ a window _____ windows
_____ a woman	_____ women	_____ a cafeteria
_____ a teacher	_____ teachers	_____ restrooms
_____ a bookcase	_____ bookcases	_____ a computer center
_____ a clock	_____ clocks	_____ a theater / an auditorium
_____ a U.S. map	_____ a world map	_____ a library
_____ a computer	_____ computers	_____ an elevator

C. In your notebook, write about your classroom and school building.

Writing Note

Edit your story. Check all the plural nouns. Remember that most plural nouns use s at the end. Check all **irregular** plural nouns such as **men** and **women**.

A. Write *a* or *an*.

1. _____ old computer
2. _____ Applied computer
3. _____ Bell computer
4. _____ English teacher
5. _____ large desk

6. _____ small table
7. _____ difficult exam
8. _____ U.S. map
9. _____ hardworking student
10. _____ auditorium

B. Change each sentence from singular to plural. Use the number in parentheses ( ).

1. There is a woman in the class (six)

   There are six women in the class.

2. There is a computer in the computer lab. (twelve)

   _____

3. There is a dictionary in my backpack. (two)

   _____

4. There is an elevator in the school. (three)

   _____

5. There is a student in Room 421. (twenty-two)

   _____

C. Complete with *There is a*, *There are*, *There is no*, or *There are no*.

1. _____ teacher is my classroom.
2. _____ students from China in my class.
3. _____ students from Central America in my class.
4. _____ computer in our classroom.
5. _____ map on the wall.
6. _____ men in our class.
7. _____ restrooms on this floor.

Looking at Numbers: The Internet

A. Look at the information in the chart.

**Percent (%) of schools
with access to the Internet**

School	1994	1997	2000
Elementary	30%	75%	97%
Secondary	49%	89%	100%

B. Read and discuss.

1. Does your school have computer labs?

2. Does your classroom have computers? How many does it have?

3. What do you use your computer for?

Grammar Summary

▶ **1. Singular nouns**

   a. Use **a** before a **consonant sound:** b c d f g h j k l m n p q r s t v w x y z
      a computer   **a d**esk

   b. Use **an** before a **vowel sound:** a e i o u   **an e**levator   **an u**gly room

   c. Be careful with nouns that begin with **u**.   **a u**niversity   **an u**mbrella

▶ **2. Plural nouns**

   a. Add **s** to make a plural noun.   eraser**s**   pen**s**   student**s**

   b. Add **es** to words that end in **-s, -ch, -sh.**   watch**es**

   c. Change **y** to **i** and add **es.**   dictionar**ies**

   d. Do <u>not</u> add an **s** to adjectives.   young student**s**

▶ **3. There is / There are / There is no / There are no**

There is a chalkboard in the classroom.

There are many students in the classroom.

There is no desk for the teacher.

There are no computers for the students in the classroom.

The Family

 Dictionary: Family Members, Occupations

 A. Listen and repeat. Then, talk about the relationships.

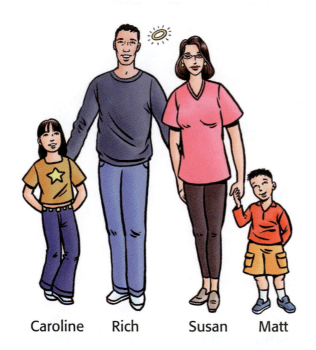

Caroline   Rich   Susan   Matt

parents	
mother	father

wife	husband

children	
daughter	son

sister	brother

 B. Listen and repeat. Then, talk about the relationships.

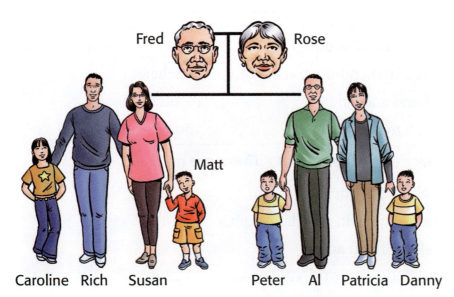

Fred   Rose

Matt

Caroline Rich Susan   Peter Al Patricia Danny

grandparents
grandmother
grandfather

grandchildren
granddaughter
grandson

aunt	uncle
niece	nephew
cousin	

C. Listen and complete.

1. Susan is Rich's _wife_____.

2. Rich is Susan's _____.

3. Caroline is Rich and Susan's _____.

4. Matt is Rich and Susan's _____.

5. Caroline is Matt's _____.

6. Susan and Rich are Caroline and Matt's _____.

7. Caroline and Matt are Susan and Rich's _____.

D. Read and answer.

1. How many grandchildren does Rose have? ____ _four grandchildren_

2. Who is Caroline's uncle? _____

3. Who are Rich's nephews? _____

4. Who is Al's father? _____

5. Who is Matt's aunt? _____

6. Who are Fred's grandsons? _____

7. How many cousins does Danny have? _____

E. Listen and repeat. Then, complete the sentences below.

mother-in-law	daughter-in-law	sister-in-law
father-in-law	son-in-law	brother-in-law

1. Fred is Patricia's **father-in-law.**
   Who is Patricia's **mother-in-law?** _____

2. Rich is Patricia's **brother-in-law.**
   Who is Patricia's **sister-in-law?** _____

3. Susan is Al's **sister.**
   Who is Al's **brother-in-law?** _____

Active Grammar: Possessive Adjectives and Possessive Nouns

A. Listen and repeat.

| my | your | his | her | our | their |

B. Listen and complete, using *she* or *her*, *he* or *his*, and *they* or *their*.

This is my little sister.

1. _____**Her**_____ name is Maria.

2. _____'s 16 years old today, but _____ birthday is next week.

3. _____ eyes are brown and _____ hair is long.

4. _____'s in tenth grade.

This is my brother.

5. _____ name is David.

6. _____'s 19 years old, and _____'s in college.

7. _____ birthday is on October 2nd.

8. _____'s a baseball player.

This is my brother, Steve, and his wife, Sue.

9. _____'re married and _____ live in Florida.

10. _____ house is in Miami.

11. _____ have two children. _____ names are Brian and Kevin.

 Personal Information

A. Read the license. Answer the questions.

DRIVER'S LICENSE
NEW MEXICO
NM2079 51562 6855

Angelica Ortega
4000 South Meadows Road
Santa Fe, New Mexico 87507

09/15/82	5'3"	Brown	10/2010
DOB	Height	Eyes	Exp. Date

Culture Note
Every driver's license has an expiration date. Your license is good for two, three, four, or more years. Then, you must renew your license.

1. What's her first name?
2. What's her last name?
3. What's her address?
4. What's her date of birth?
5. How old is she?
6. What is her height?
7. What color are her eyes?
8. What is the expiration date?

B. My classmates. Write the name of a classmate who matches the description. Then complete the sentence, using *his* or *her*.

long hair

short hair

wavy hair

curly hair

1. _____Maria's_____ hair is black.   ____Her____ hair is black.
2. _____ eyes are brown.   _____ eyes are brown.
3. _____ hair is brown.   _____ hair is brown.
4. _____ eyes are blue.   _____ eyes are blue.
5. _____ eyes are large.   _____ eyes are large.
6. _____ hair is long.   _____ hair is long.
7. _____ hair is curly.   _____ hair is curly.
8. _____ hair is wavy.   _____ hair is wavy.
9. _____ hair is short.   _____ hair is short.

 Occupations

A. Read the occupations. Ask your teacher about any new words.

an accountant	a cook	an engineer	landscapers
an auto mechanic	a custodian	factory workers	a waiter / a waitress

B. Write the occupations under the correct pictures.

1. _____ 2. _____ 3. _____

4. _____ 5. _____ 6. _____

7. _____ 8. _____ 9. _____

C. *A and An.* Put *a* or *an* before each occupation.

1. __a__ nurse 4. _____ doctor 7. _____ busy accountant

2. _____ landscaper 5. _____ teacher 8. _____ tired waitress

3. _____ excellent cook 6. _____ student 9. _____ electrical engineer

 More Occupations

A. Read the occupations. Ask your teacher about any new words.

an architect	a farmer	a nurse
an artist	a home health aide	a secretary
a bus driver	a housewife	a security guard
a computer programmer	a lawyer	a taxi driver
a dentist	a machine operator	a travel agent

B. Write three occupations under each workplace.

Factory

Office

Hospital

a machine operator

Restaurant

School

Outdoors

C. Complete the sentences about your family.

1. My _____brother_____ , _____Massimo_____ , is __a__ _____dentist_____ .
            family member   name   a / an   occupation

2. My _____ , _____ , is _____ _____ .

3. My _____ , _____ , is _____ _____ .

4. My _____ , _____ , is _____ _____ .

5. My _____ , _____ , is _____ _____ .

A. Pronunciation: *What's*. Listen and repeat.

1. What's her name?
2. What's her address?
3. What's your name?
4. What's your last name?
5. What's his name?

6. What's his address?
7. What's her job?
8. What's your job?
9. What's her first name?
10. What's his name?

 B. Listen and complete.

1. What's _____ name?
2. What's _____ name?
3. What's _____ address?

4. What's _____ address?
5. What's _____ job?
6. What's _____ job?

 Practice the questions with a partner.

Working Together: Student to Student

A. STUDENT A: Cover the questions. Look at the picture of the family. Then, listen to Student B and answer the questions.

STUDENT B: Read the questions about the family to Student A. Student A will answer the questions.

Masa   Yoko   Hiro   Julia   Loretta

Eddie   Yoshiko

1. Who is Julia's husband?
2. Who is Yoshiko's brother?
3. Who is Masa's daughter-in-law?
4. Who is Eddie's grandmother?
5. Who is Julia's mother-in-law?
6. Who is Loretta's niece?
7. Who is Masa's grandson?
8. Who is Hiro's daughter?
9. Who is Eddie's aunt?

B. Photographs. Two students, Beata and Olga, are talking about their photographs. With a partner, read and practice the conversation.

Beata: These are my children, Peter and Zofia. Peter is 6 and Zofia is 5.

Olga: Are they in school?

Beata: Peter is in first grade, and Zofia is in kindergarten. And, how about you?

Olga: I have a little girl. This is her picture. Her name is Maria.

Beata: She's beautiful. How old is she?

Olga: She's four years old.

Beata: She looks like you. She has your eyes and nose.

C. Your Family. Bring in one or two photographs of your family. Write a conversation with a partner. Use these questions and expressions.

Who's this?	Who's this?
What's his name?	What's her name?
How old is he?	How old is she?
Is he in school?	Is she in school?
What's his occupation?	What's her occupation?
He looks like you.	She looks like you.
He looks like his father.	She looks like her father.
He has your eyes / nose / hair.	She has your eyes / nose / hair.

The Big Picture: A Family Reunion

A. Talk about the picture.

1. Where is the family?

2. What is the occasion?

3. What do you think the family relationships are?

 B. Listen and label the family members.

Betty	Frank	Erika
Julia	Bobby, Jr.	Valerie

C. Read and complete about the family in Exercise A.

1. Victoria has four children, _____, _____, _____, and _____.

2. Bobby and _____ are married. They have two children, _____ and _____.

3. Benita's children are _____ and _____.

4. Victor and Valerie are _____ .

5. Bobby, Jr., is holding his _____, Erika. Erika is Victor and Valerie's _____.

D. Match each person with an occupation.

1. Julia works in a hospital.   a. He's a mail carrier.

2. Betty works with food.   b. She's a bus driver.

3. Bobby works for the post office.   c. She's a homemaker.

4. Benita drives a bus.   d. He's retired.

5. Victoria is 70 years old. She doesn't work.   e. She's a doctor.

6. Barbara stays at home with her children.   f. She's a cook.

7. Frank is 73. He doesn't work.   g. She's retired.

E. Complete the sentences. Use the possessive 's form.

1. Frank is _____ *Victoria's* _____ husband.

2. Frank is _____ father.

3. Bobby, Jr. is _____ grandson.

4. Erika is _____ sister.

5. Victor and Valerie are _____ children.

6. Barbara, Betty, and Benita are _____ sisters.

7. Julia is _____ daughter-in-law.

8. Barbara is _____ sister-in-law.

9. Bobby, Jr. and Erika are _____ cousins.

A. Before You Read.

How many people are in your family? Are you married or single?

Family 1: A Nuclear Family

This is my family. I live with my husband and my two children. My husband's parents live an hour away. We visit the grandparents on holidays, in the summer, and sometimes on the weekends.

Family 2: An Extended Family

This is my family. I live with my parents, my wife and my two children. My parents are both 70 years old. They're retired. My daughter is 14 years old. She's in high school. My son is 9 years old. He's in 4th grade.

Family 3: A Blended Family

This is my family. I was married before, and my wife, Linda, was too. Her first husband died. My first wife and I divorced. Linda has two children from her first marriage. I have one child from my first marriage.

B. Read and check (✓) what is true about the families in Exercise A.

	Family 1	Family 2	Family 3
1. There are three children in this family.			
2. The children live with their parents and grandparents.			
3. The daughter-in-law lives with her mother-in-law.			
4. The grandparents live in a different house.			
5. The parents have children from different relationships.			
6. My family is similar to . . .			

Writing Our Stories: My Family

A. Read.

My name is Luis. This is a photo of me, my wife, and some of our grandchildren. My wife and I have 11 grandsons and three granddaughters. The oldest is 15 years old, and the youngest is nine months old. Ten of our grandchildren live here in the United States. One of our sons still lives in Colombia. He's married and has one child. We visit them once a year.

B. Complete.

1. I am **single / married / divorced.**

2. My **wife's / husband's** name is _____.

   He's / She's a / an _____.

3. I have _____ children. **My daughter's name / My son's name**

   is _____.

4. My mother's name is _____. She's _____ years old.

5. My father's name is _____. He's _____ years old.

6. I am **a / an** _____.

C. In your notebook, write about your family.

Writing Note

Edit your story.
Remember to use 's with possessives:
Frank's daughter

A. Answer the questions about yourself.

1. What's your first name?   <u>My first name is . . .</u> _____

2. What's your last name?   _____

3. What's your date of birth?   _____

4. What's your occupation?   _____

5. What color is your hair?   _____

6. What color are your eyes?   _____

7. What's your mother's name?   _____

8. What's your father's name?   _____

B. The Campbell family. Read carefully and complete the story. Use *he, she, they, their, his, her,* and *is* or *are.*

The Campbell family lives in Chicago, Illinois. The father's name __<u>is</u>__

Robert, and the mother's name _____ Ginger. Robert's job is

interesting. _____ _____ a police officer. _____

wife has an unusual job for a woman. She _____ an auto

mechanic. _____ have three children, Leslie, Louis, and Melanie.

Leslie _____ 10 years old, Louis _____ 9 years old, and

Melanie _____ 6 years old. _____ _____

elementary school students. _____ grandmother lives in the

house, too. _____ name is Matilda. The family has a dog, too.

_____ dog's name is Friendly.

Looking at Graphs: American Households

A. Talk about the graph.

household — the people who live together in one home

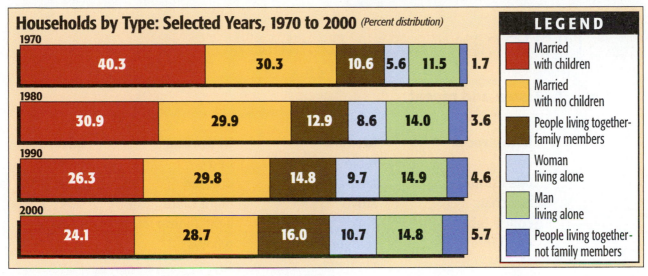

Households by Type: Selected Years, 1970 to 2000 *(Percent distribution)*

1970	40.3	30.3	10.6	5.6	11.5	1.7
1980	30.9	29.9	12.9	8.6	14.0	3.6
1990	26.3	29.8	14.8	9.7	14.9	4.6
2000	24.1	28.7	16.0	10.7	14.8	5.7

LEGEND
- Married with children
- Married with no children
- People living together—family members
- Woman living alone
- Man living alone
- People living together—not family members

Source: U.S. Census 2000.

B. Where do you belong in the graph?

Grammar Summary

> **1. Possessive nouns**   Add apostrophe *s* (**'s**).

David is **Olga's** husband.

That is **Tom's** book.

David is **Tom and Kathy's** father.

> **2. Possessive adjectives**   Use a possessive adjective before a noun.

I	→	**My** class is at 9:00.
You	→	**Your** hair is long and wavy.
He	→	**His** eyes are brown.
She	→	**Her** eyes are blue.
We	→	**Our** teacher is friendly.
They	→	**Their** classroom is large.

Home and Neighborhood

Dictionary: Rooms, Furniture

A. Listen and repeat.

living room	kitchen	bedroom	bathroom
sofa	table	bed	bathtub
television/TV	chairs	dresser	toilet
armchair	stove	night table	sink
coffee table	sink	light / lamp	shower
end table	refrigerator	pillows	
picture	cabinets		
	counter		

B. Label the furniture in this house.

Active Grammar: Prepositions

in	on	next to	between	under	over	in front of	in back of / behind

1.

2.

3.

4.

5.

6.

7.

8.

D. Complete. Look at the picture on page 60 and complete.

1. The sofa is ____in____ the living room.

2. The end table is _____ the sofa.

3. The book is _____ the coffee table.

4. The lamp is _____ the end table.

5. The picture is _____ the sofa.

6. The dresser is _____ the bedroom.

7. The night table is _____ the bed and the dresser.

8. The light is _____ the bed.

9. The table is _____ the kitchen.

10. The toilet is _____ the bathtub.

11. The mirror is _____ the dresser.

12. The cabinets are _____ the refrigerator.

13. The clock is _____ the lamp.

14. The pillows are _____ the bed.

E. Answer. Look at the picture on page 60 and answer.

> **Where is the end table?**
> It's next to the sofa.

> **Where are the books?**
> They're on the coffee table.

1. Where is the television?

2. Where is the refrigerator?

3. Where is the picture?

4. Where are the pillows?

5. Where is the night table?

6. Where are the cabinets?

7. Where is the dresser?

8. Where is the toilet?

9. Where is the bathtub?

10. Where is the stove?

Where's my soccer ball?

A. Bob's room is always a mess. He's asking his mother about each item. Listen and write the number of each location.

a. telephone   __4__

b. wallet   _____

c. keys   _____

d. soccer ball   _____

e. backpack   _____

f. sneakers   _____

B. Complete these conversations about the picture.

1. **Bob:** Mom, where's my tennis racquet?

   Mom: I think it's _____.

2. **Bob:** Mom, where_____ my radio?

   Mom: I think it's _____.

3. **Bob:** Mom, where_____ my baseball hat?

   Mom: Look _____.

4. **Bob:** Mom, where_____ my books?

   Mom: Look _____.

C. The classroom. Look around your classroom and answer these questions with a partner.

1. Where is the door?

2. Where are the windows?

3. Where is the clock?

4. Where is the chalkboard?

5. Where is the map?

6. Where is the wastepaper basket?

7. Where is the pencil sharpener?

8. Where is the teacher?

9. Where is the teacher's desk?

10. Where are you?

 Furniture

A. Megan's new apartment. Megan is moving into her first apartment today. What does she have? What does she need?

> She has a computer.   She needs a desk.

 B. Interview. Ask your partner these questions. (Circle) the answer.

1. Do you have a stereo?   Yes, I do.   No, I don't.
2. Do you have a computer?   Yes, I do.   No, I don't.
3. Do you have a desk?   Yes, I do.   No, I don't.
4. Do you have a VCR or a DVD?   Yes, I do.   No, I don't.
5. Do you have a microwave?   Yes, I do.   No, I don't.
6. Do you have a cell phone?   Yes, I do.   No, I don't.
7. Do you have a pager?   Yes, I do.   No, I don't.
8. Do you have a fax machine?   Yes, I do.   No, I don't.

C. Complete.

1. My partner has a _____.
2. My partner has a _____.
3. My partner needs a _____.
4. I have a _____.
5. I have a _____.
6. I need a _____.

> *Have/Has*
> I **have** a computer.
> He **has** a computer.
> She **has** a computer.

Dictionary: My Neighborhood

A. Listen and repeat.

department store	drugstore	bank	diner
supermarket	library	jewelry store	police station
laundromat	post office	barber shop	bookstore
car wash	parking lot	City Hall	hospital

B. Write the names of six more stores or buildings in a town.

_____   _____

_____   _____

_____   _____

C. Complete with the name of a store or building.

1. I can mail a letter at the _post office_____.

2. I can wash my car at the _____.

3. I can get a prescription at the _____.

4. I can eat lunch at the _____.

5. I can borrow a book at the _____.

6. I can get emergency medical help at the _____.

7. I can wash my clothes at the _____.

8. I can buy a coat at the _____.

9. I can buy food at the _____.

10. I can get a marriage license at _____.

11. I can get help at the _____.

12. I can get a haircut at the _____.

13. I can buy a book or a magazine at _____.

14. I can park my car in the _____.

15. I can _____.

D. Read.

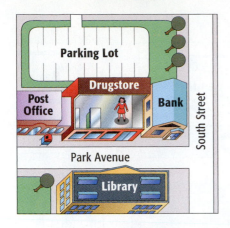

The drugstore is on Park Avenue.
Jenny is **in** the drugstore.
The drugstore is **next to** the post office.
The drugstore is **between** the post office and the bank.
The bank is **on the corner of** Park Avenue and South Street.
The drugstore is **across from** the library.
The parking lot is **in back of** the drugstore.
The mailbox is **in front of** the post office.

E. Read the sentences below and write each store or building on the map.

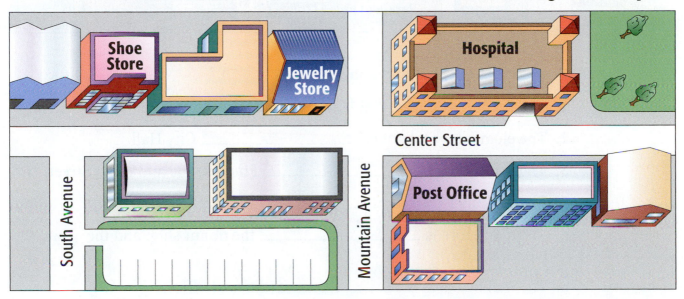

1. The laundromat is between the shoe store and the jewelry store.

2. The park is next to the hospital.

3. The bank is across from the park.

4. The bus station is on the corner of Center Street and South Avenue.

5. The diner is between the post office and the bank.

6. The drugstore is next to the shoe store.

7. The police station is next to the bus station.

8. The library is on Mountain Avenue, next to the post office.

9. The parking lot is in back of the bus station.

 Downtown

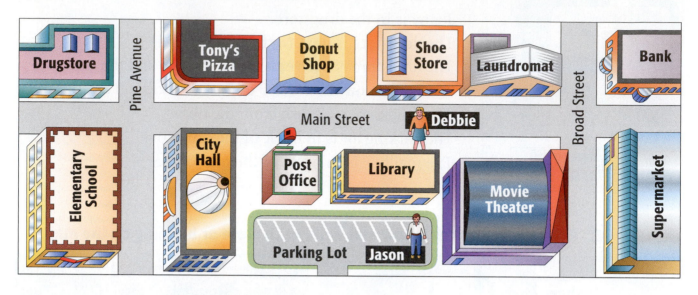

A. Complete about the map above.

1. The library is _____*next to*_____ the post office.

2. The elementary school is _____ City Hall.

3. The drugstore is _____ Pine Avenue and Main Street.

4. The parking lot is _____ the library.

5. The shoe store is _____ the donut shop and the laundromat.

6. The mailbox is _____ the post office.

7. Jason is _____ the parking lot.

8. The donut shop is _____ Main Street.

B. Complete these conversations about the map above.

1. **A:** Where's the bank?

   B: It's _____.

2. **A:** Where's the supermarket?

   B: It's _____.

3. **A:** Where's Debbie?

   B: It's _____.

 C. Talk about the location of each building on the map above.

D. Pronunciation. Prepositions: *in back of, in front of.* Listen and repeat.

1. The pizza shop is in back of the supermarket.
2. The mailbox is in front of the post office.

> in front of — in front_of
> in back of — in back_of

3. The parking lot is in back of the school.
4. The flag is in front of City Hall.
5. The children are in front of the school.

 Practice these sentences with a partner.

Working Together: Student to Student

A. STUDENT A: Look at the map below. Ask Student B about the location of the places in the box. Complete the map.

STUDENT B: Do not look at your partner's map! Turn to page 68.

the Mexican restaurant	the supermarket	the diner
the bus station	the police station	the bakery

> Where's the Mexican restaurant?

> It's on the corner of River Road and Second Street.

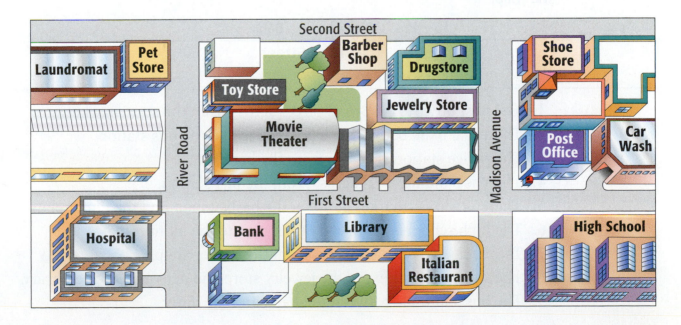

Working Together: Student to Student

B. STUDENT B: Look at the map below. Ask Student A about the location of the places in the box. Do not look at your partner's map! Complete the map.

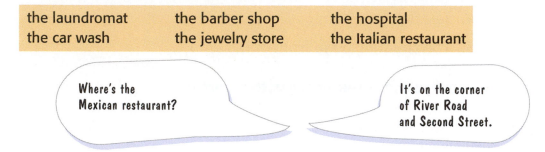

| the laundromat | the barber shop | the hospital |
| the car wash | the jewelry store | the Italian restaurant |

Where's the Mexican restaurant?

It's on the corner of River Road and Second Street.

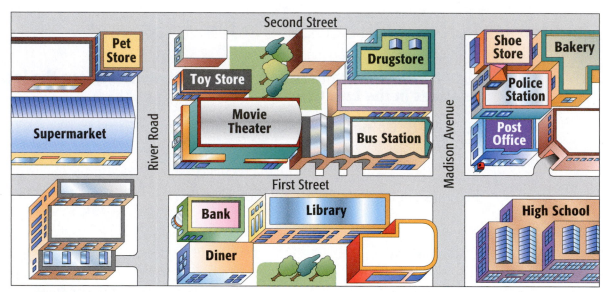

C. Figure it out! Read the location of each store. Write the names of the stores on the map.

		Post Office	Bank		

Broad Street

		Supermarket			

1. The post office is on Broad Street across from the supermarket.
2. There is a bank between the post office and the bus station.
3. The police station is across from the bank.
4. There is a laundromat across from the bus station.
5. There is a supermarket between the barber shop and the police station.
6. The high school is on Broad Street next to the laundromat.
7. There's a jewelry store across from the barber shop.
8. The shoe store is next to the jewelry store and across from the library.
9. The bus station is between the bank and the diner.

C. Downtown. Sit with a partner. Plan a town. Include the stores and buildings in the box. Add more stores and buildings. Name the streets.

elementary school	high school	library	bank
post office	shoe store	music store	bookstore
drugstore	beauty parlor	car wash	pizza shop
_____	_____	_____	_____

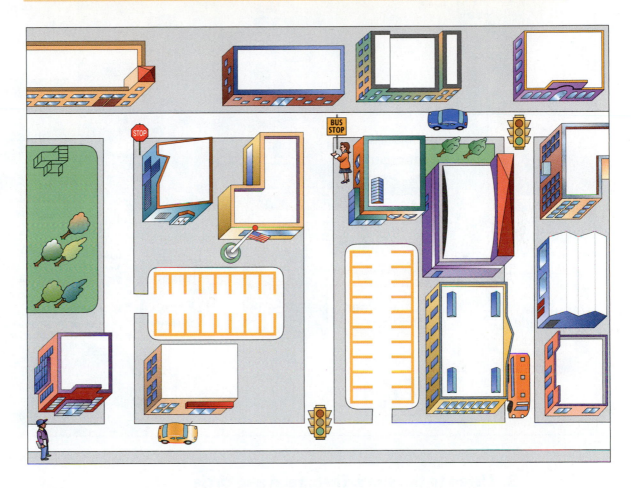

D. Write five sentences about the locations of the buildings on your map.

1. _____
2. _____
3. _____
4. _____
5. _____

The Big Picture: Pine Street

A. Talk about the location of the buildings in this neighborhood.

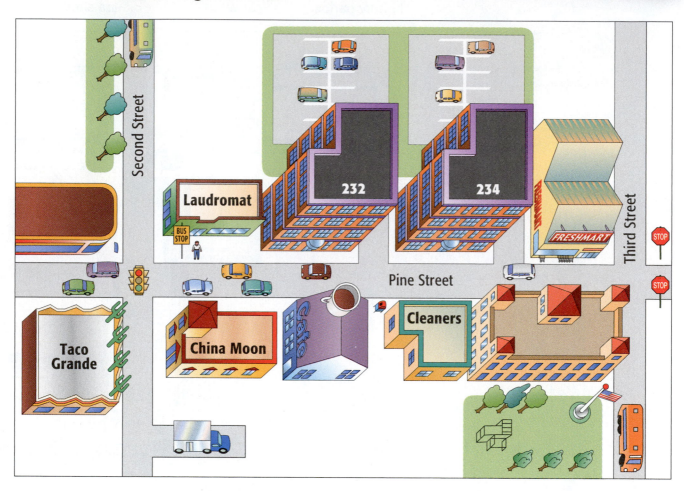

B. Listen to the story. Then, read and circle.

1.	Magda lives at 238 Pine Street.	Yes	No
2.	She lives in a one-bedroom apartment.	Yes	No
3.	She has two children.	Yes	No
4.	Her children go to the school across the street.	Yes	No
5.	Her sister lives in the same building.	Yes	No
6.	There is a laundry room on the first floor of the building.	Yes	No
7.	Her husband drives to work.	Yes	No
8.	The neighbors are friendly.	Yes	No

C. Complete with a preposition.

1. I live _____in_____ a small apartment building on Pine Street.

2. My sister lives in the building _____ me.

3. The coffee shop is _____ the apartment building.

4. The Mexican restaurant is _____ the Chinese restaurant.

5. The bus stop is _____ the laundromat.

6. The cleaners is _____ the coffee shop and the school.

7. The park is _____ the school.

8. The parking lot is _____ the apartment buildings.

9. The school is _____ Pine Street and Third Street.

10. The grocery store is _____ my sister's apartment building.

D. Complete. Use *can* and a verb from the list.

1. My husband _____can get_____ the bus on the corner.

2. My daughters _____ to school.

3. I _____ a cup of coffee across the street.

4. I _____ my sister every day.

5. I _____ my clothes at the laundromat.

6. I _____ in back of the building.

7. My daughters _____ in the park.

> play
> buy
> visit
> wash
> ✓get
> park
> walk

E. Listen and respond to each statement. Use *That's good* or *That's too bad.*

1. That's good. _____

2. That's too bad. _____

3. _____

4. _____

5. _____

6. _____

7. _____

8. _____

9. _____

10. _____

A. Before You Read. Imagine that you are very rich. You are going to build a house. What will you put in your house?

☐ a swimming pool   ☐ an office   ☐ an exercise room

☐ a spa   ☐ a guest room   ☐ a library

☐ a five-car garage   ☐ _____

Bill Gates is the president of Microsoft, the largest computer software company in the world. He is the richest person in the United States. Microsoft is located in Seattle, Washington. In 1990, Bill Gates decided to build a house on Lake Washington, near Seattle.

At first, Bill Gates wanted a small house. He was single. He wanted a house with a kitchen, a dining room, a living room, and three bedrooms. But, in planning, Gates had many ideas. Also, in 1994, Gates got married. His wife, Melinda, had more ideas.

It took seven years to build the Gates' house. It doesn't have six rooms. It has 20 rooms! There is an indoor swimming pool; the pool is 60 feet long. You can listen to music underwater when you swim. You can watch a movie in the 20-seat theater. One hundred people can sit in the dining room. There is an exercise room, two spas, and a sauna. In the main reception room, there is a 24-monitor video wall. The garage is very large; there are spaces for 30 cars! There is a guest house for friends. And, there is a boat house on the lake.

Bill and Melinda Gates now have two children. They need more room, so it's time to expand the house!

B. Write the name of the room.

1. One hundred people can eat in the _____.
2. You can swim in the _____.
3. You can read a book in the _____.
4. You can relax in the _____.
5. You can park your car in the _____.
6. You can watch a movie in the _____.
7. Friends can stay in the _____.

C. Underline these words in the story. What is the meaning of each word?

| lake | underwater | reception | guest | expand |

Writing Our Stories: My Neighborhood

A. Read.

I live in Oakland, California. I am from China, and there are many people from China in my neighborhood. I live in an apartment near the town. There are many Chinese stores on my street. There is a Chinese grocery store across from my apartment building. I can buy my favorite kinds of Chinese fruit, such as lichee and duran. Every Friday I buy the Chinese newspapers there. There is a good video store on the corner. I can rent movies from the United States and from China. There are many Chinese restaurants. Some of the restaurants have very good food. There is a bank next to my apartment building. The tellers speak English and Chinese. My street is always busy, but on Saturday and Sunday, it is very busy.

B. Name six buildings or stores in your neighborhood.

_____   _____

_____   _____

_____   _____

C. Write about your neighborhood.

I live in _____, _____. I live
                 city   state
in **a house / an apartment** on _____ Street. My neighborhood
is quiet / busy.

_____

_____

_____

_____

_____

Writing Note
Street names begin with capital letters: Main Street.

Practicing on Your Own

A. Prepositions. Look at this map. Complete the sentences.

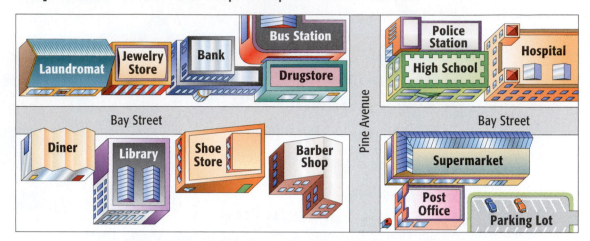

1. The bank is _____between_____ the jewelry store and the drugstore.

2. There is a bus station _____ the police station.

3. The high school is _____ Pine Avenue and Bay Street.

4. The library is _____ Bay Street.

5. The barber shop is _____ Pine Avenue and Bay Street.

6. The parking lot is _____ the supermarket.

7. There is a jewelry store _____ the laundromat.

8. The hospital is _____ the high school.

9. There is a shoe store _____ the bank.

10. The shoe store is _____ the barber shop and the library.

B. Complete. Use *can* and a verb from the list.

1. I _____can get_____ a prescription at the drugstore.

2. I _____ sneakers at the shoe store.

3. I _____ a haircut at the barber shop.

4. I _____ a letter at the post office.

5. I _____ a check at the bank.

6. I _____ a book at the library.

7. I _____ breakfast at the diner.

can mail
can eat
can buy
can get
✓can get
can cash
can borrow

Looking at Charts: Electronic Equipment

A. Look at the chart. It shows the percentage of homes in the United States with different kinds of electronic equipment. Look at the chart and complete the sentences.

1. Most homes have a _____.

2. Many homes have a _____.

3. Half of the homes have a _____.

4. Not many homes have a _____.

5. I have a _____.

6. I would like a _____.

Electronic Equipment	
Television	98%
Radio	98%
Telephone	96%
VCR	88%
Answering machine	60%
Computer	50%
Cell phone	33%
Camcorder	23%
Fax machine	8%

Grammar Summary

▶ 1. Prepositions

The keys are **in** the desk.

The keys are **on** the table.

The keys are **next to** the telephone.

The keys are **between** the telephone and the lamp.

The keys are **under** the chair.

The jewelry store is **on** Park Avenue.

The bank is **next to** the drugstore.

The supermarket is **across from** the police station.

The bakery is **between** the shoe store and the post office.

The diner is **on the corner of** Main Street and Park Avenue.

The parking lot is **in back of** / **behind** the supermarket.

The mailbox is **in front of** the post office.

▶ 2. *Can*

I **can wash** my clothes at the laundromat.

I **can buy** stamps at the post office.

6 A Typical Day

Dictionary: Daily Activities

A. Listen and repeat. Then, complete the sentences.

brushes	eats	gets	leaves	runs	takes
drives	gets	gets up	makes	shaves	wakes up

1. Hugo _____wakes up_____ at 6:30 A.M.

2. He _____.

3. He _____ from 7:00 A.M. to 7:30 A.M.

4. He _____ a shower.

5. He _____.

6. He _____ dressed for work.

7. He _____ coffee.

8. He _____ breakfast.

9. He _____ his teeth.

10. He _____ the house.

11. He _____ to work.

12. He _____ to work at 8:50 A.M.

B. **Listen and repeat. Then, complete the sentences.**

eats	goes	makes	walks	washes	watches

1. Rosa _____ home.

2. She _____ her dog.

3. She _____ dinner.

4. She _____ dinner.

5. She _____ the dishes.

6. She _____ TV.

C. **Listen and repeat. Then, complete the sentences.**

do	eat	go	play	take	watch

1. David and Sofia _____ the bus.

2. They _____ their homework.

3. They _____ outside.

4. They _____ dinner.

5. They _____ TV.

6. They _____ to bed.

Active Grammar: Present Tense

A. Complete about your schedule.

1. I wake up at _____.

2. I get up at _____.

3. I eat breakfast at _____.

4. I **drive / walk / take the bus** to work at _____.

5. I arrive at **work / school** at _____.

6. I go home at _____.

7. I do homework at _____.

> I wake up at 6:30.
> I go to bed at 11:00.

B. Complete with verbs from the list.

1. Hugo _____*gets up*_____ at 6:30.

2. His children _____ at 7:00.

3. Hugo _____ in the park every morning.

4. Hugo _____ to work at 8:00.

5. David and Sofia _____ the bus at 8:10.

6. Rosa _____ to work.

7. David and Sofia _____ TV from 8:00 to 9:30.

8. Rosa _____ TV from 9:00 to 10:30.

9. The family _____ dinner together every night.

10. The children _____ lunch at school.

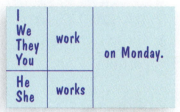

I We They You	work	on Monday.
He She	works	

drive
drives
eat
eats
get up
✓ gets up
run
runs
take
takes
watch
watches
walk
walks

 Time Expressions

A. Look at the chart. Use your imagination. Talk about Hugo and his family's schedules. Then, talk about your schedule.

I Hugo and Rosa	exercise eat dinner go to work watch the news visit friends	at _____ : _____. on weekends. in the morning. in the evening. every day. from Monday to Friday.
Sofia David	does homework eats lunch plays outside watches TV goes to bed	

 B. More time expressions. Ask and answer questions with a partner.

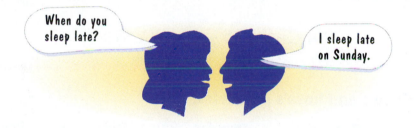

When do you sleep late?

I sleep late on Sunday.

on
on Monday
on Friday
on weekends

in
in the morning
in the afternoon
in the evening
in the summer
in the winter

1. When do you sleep late?

2. When do you take a vacation?

3. When do you watch TV?

4. When do you go to school?

5. When do you do laundry?

6. When do you go to the grocery store?

7. When do you go to the beach?

8. When do you have a barbecue?

9. When do you watch the news?

10. When do you go to bed?

 Negatives

| I We You They | don't do not | work sleep late drink coffee get up early | on weekends. on Sunday. on weekdays. in the evening. |
| He She It | doesn't does not | | |

A. Complete the sentences, using a time expression.

1. I don't go to school _on Sunday_____.

2. I don't get up early _____.

3. I don't sleep late _____.

4. I don't go to the grocery store _____.

5. I don't drink coffee or tea _____.

6. I don't go to bed late _____.

 Compare your sentences with a partner. Then, talk about your partner's habits.

My partner doesn't go to school on Sunday.

B. Talk about Hugo's and Rosa's schedules.

C. Complete the sentences about Hugo and Rosa.

eat
✓ work
study
stay
go

1. Rosa _____works_____ on Wednesday.

2. Hugo ____doesn't work____ on Thursdays.

3. Hugo _____ to the gym on Thursdays.

4. Hugo _____ on Thursday evenings.

5. Rosa and Hugo _____ to school on Wednesday evenings.

6. Rosa _____ on Friday mornings.

   She _____ to the gym.

With a partner, write eight more sentences about Hugo's and Rosa's schedules. Four sentences must be negative.

D. Cultural differences. Read the statements about American culture. Then, talk about your culture.

> Americans drive everywhere.
> Russians don't drive everywhere. They use public transportation.
>   or
> In Russia, we do, too.

1. Americans use credit cards.

2. Americans use babysitters.

3. Americans shop at shopping malls.

4. Americans move many times.

5. Americans watch many hours of TV.

6. Americans like football.

7. American teenagers wear jeans to school.

8. Americans eat a large meal in the evening.

Write five more cultural differences.

Writing Note
Countries and nationalities begin with capital letters: Russia, Brazilians.

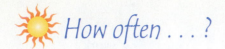

How often . . . ?

A. Adverbs of frequency. Complete the sentences with adverbs.

1. I _____ go to school.

2. I _____ speak English in class.

3. I _____ do my homework.

4. I _____ eat breakfast.

5. I am _____ late for an appointment.

6. I am _____ on time for class.

7. I am _____ nervous before an exam.

8. I am _____ relaxed.

100%	always
80%	usually
50%	sometimes
0%	never

B. Ask your partner these questions.

once — one time

twice — two times

1. How often do you exercise?

2. How often do you play a sport?

3. How often do you wash your car?

4. How often do you visit your native country?

5. How often do you go to the park?

6. How often do you eat out?

once a week
once a month
twice a week
twice a month
three times a week
every day
every morning
every evening
every night
every summer
every year
*never (*Look at Exercise A.)

C. Work with a partner. Write three more *How often* questions, and ask the teacher your questions.

A. Pronunciation: Final *s*. Listen and repeat.

/ s /	/ z /	/ əs /
wakes	drives	fixes
walks	arrives	relaxes
takes	does	washes
drinks	goes	brushes
likes	knows	watches
eats	plays	
gets	wears	
sleeps		
shops		

B. Read the verbs. Pronounce them. Put them in the correct columns.
Add two or more verbs to each column.

/ s /	/ z /	/ əs /

cleans
studies
finishes
leaves
stops
cooks
teaches
speaks
buys
visits
practices

Practice saying the verbs with a partner.

 Working Together

A. Interview. Work with a partner. Ask and answer these questions. Write the time.

Question	You	Your partner
What time do you get up?		
What time do you leave for school?		
What time do you get home from school?		
What hours do you work?		
What time do you eat dinner?		
What time do you do your homework?		
What time do you go to sleep?		
What time do you get up on weekends?		

B. More about the interview. Look at your chart. Circle the correct information about the schedules.

1. My partner gets up **early / late.**

2. I **get up / don't get up** early.

3. My partner **leaves / doesn't leave** for school early in the morning.

4. I **leave / don't leave** for school at about the same time.

5. My partner **works / doesn't work.**

6. I **work / don't work.**

7. My partner does homework in **the morning / the afternoon / the evening.**

8. I do my homework in **the morning / the afternoon / the evening.**

9. My partner **goes / doesn't go** to bed before midnight.

C. My day. The teacher will give each student 10 small pieces of paper. On each piece of paper, write an activity that you do on a typical day, such as:

Then, give the pieces of paper to a partner. Describe your typical day. Your partner will listen and arrange your papers in the correct order. You cannot touch the papers!

| First,
Next,
Then,
After that, | *First, I exercise from 6:30 to 7:00. Then, I take a shower. I eat breakfast at 7:30 in the morning. Next, I brush my teeth. After that, I study.* |

D. A day in the life. In a small group, think of a famous person. Choose an athlete, an actress, a politician, a singer, a writer, etc. What is a typical day for this famous person? Write six sentences describing a day in the life of this person. Use your imagination!

> 1. Michael Jordan gets up at 10:00.
> 2. He goes to the gym.
> 3. He plays basketball.
> 4. He talks to his family.

1. _____
2. _____
3. _____
4. _____
5. _____
6. _____

Tell your classmates about *A day in the life of (the famous person)*.

The Big Picture: A Daily Schedule

A. Listen to Susan's and Peter's schedules. Write the correct time on each clock. Then, talk about their schedules.

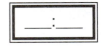

B. Complete the sentences about Susan's and Peter's schedules. Use the simple present tense.

drink	drive	eat	✓get	go	run	walk	watch	work

1. Susan and Peter _____get_____ up early.

2. Susan _____ for 30 minutes.

3. They _____ breakfast together.

4. Susan _____ a healthy breakfast.

5. Peter always _____ coffee.

6. Peter _____ to work.

7. Susan _____ to work.

8. Susan and Peter _____ from 9:00 to 5:00.

9. They _____ to classes twice a week.

10. Peter _____ TV in the evening.

C. Correct it! The information is not correct. Find the mistakes. Then, say the sentences correctly.

> Susan takes a shower first.
> Susan **doesn't take** a shower first.
> Peter **takes** a shower first.

> They leave for work at 9:00.
> They **don't leave** for work at 9:00.
> They **leave** for work at 8:00.

1. Susan and Peter get up at 8:00.

2. They eat breakfast at 7:00.

3. Peter drinks tea for breakfast.

4. Peter runs in the morning.

5. Peter eats yogurt for breakfast.

6. Susan drives to work.

7. Susan works at a construction company.

8. They go to bed at midnight.

D. A daily schedule. Look at the pictures of Susan's and Peter's schedules. In your notebook, write a story about their schedules.

Reading: A Day at the Bakery

A. Before You Read.

1. Where do you buy bread?
2. What do you buy at a bakery?
3. Where is the best bakery in your neighborhood?

It's 3:00 A.M. Angela is ready to start the day at the family bakery. She has three children, and they all help at the bakery. Vincent and Angela are the owners of his family's bakery. Vincent's father owned the bakery, and before that, Vincent's grandfather owned the bakery. Now, Vincent and his wife, Angela, own and manage the bakery.

Everyone in the family works in the bakery. The oldest daughter, Claire, decorates many of the special cakes. Maria is the middle child. She works at the counter, and sometimes she makes cookies. Paul is only 14, but he makes bread. Vincent says, "Paul has good hands for bread." The whole family works in the bakery, but the children only work there before or after school.

Mr. Martino is a regular customer. He visits the bakery every morning. He always buys the round loaf of bread with no seeds. He says that it's good. Mrs. Salerno is also a regular customer. Every Friday, she buys two loaves of Italian bread and a large box of cookies. Her six-year-old daughter, Laura, always gets one free cookie. Mrs. Salerno says that Vincent's bakery is the best in the area.

The bakery is open from 6:30 A.M. to 3:00 P.M. every day except Monday. The bakery sells cookies, cakes, and bread. For special holidays, such as Easter and Christmas, Vincent keeps the bakery open until 6:00 P.M., and Angela always prepares fresh coffee for their customers.

B. Circle the answer.

1.	Angela goes to work at 6:00 A.M.	Yes	No
2.	Angela and her husband manage the bakery.	Yes	No
3.	The children work in the bakery all day.	Yes	No
4.	Claire usually makes bread.	Yes	No
5.	Paul makes bread and cakes.	Yes	No
6.	Mr. Martino goes to the bakery every day.	Yes	No
7.	Mrs. Salerno buys cakes and cookies every week.	Yes	No
8.	The bakery is open every day.	Yes	No

Writing Our Stories: My Day

A. Read.

I am from Colombia. I came to the United States eight years ago. In Colombia, I had a deli. I made all kinds of sandwiches, hamburgers, hot dogs, and Colombian dishes. Now, I have a job in a Cuban bakery. A friend told me about the job. I didn't have any experience, but now I have a lot of experience.

I have a difficult schedule. On Saturday, Sunday, and Monday, I work from 4:00 A.M. to 3:00 P.M. I bake all kinds of breads: garlic bread, butter bread, bread with cheese, and special bread with pork inside. On Tuesday, Wednesday, and Thursday I work from 10:00 A.M. to 7:00 P.M. I help customers at the counter. From 7:30 P.M. to 10:00 P.M., I study English four nights a week. I get home at about 10:30 P.M. Then, I take a shower and do my homework. I'm very busy, but I like my job. In the future I would like to have my own bakery.

Patricia, Colombia

B. Complete the sentences with information about yourself.

1. I get up at _____.
   time

2. I **drive / walk / take public transportation** to work.

3. I get to work at _____. I work at _____.
   time   company name

4. I work from _____ to _____.
   time   time

5. I go to school on _____.
   days of the week

6. I get home from school at _____.
   time

C. In your notebook, write a story about your typical day.

> **Writing Note**
>
> Put **time** expressions at the beginning or at the end of a sentence.
>
> **On Monday,** I don't go to work.
>
> I don't go to work **on Monday.**

A. Put the words in the correct order. Write the sentences.

1. in the morning / I / drink / orange juice / always

   <u>I always drink orange juice in the morning.</u>

2. every / Mrs. Salerno / her / go / to the bakery / and / daughter / Friday

   _____

3. holidays / to school / don't / the students / on / go

   _____

4. twice / takes / an / a / she / class / week / English

   _____

5. exercise / gym / to / 6:00 A.M. / they / at / from / 7:30 A.M. / the

   _____

B. Read the sentences. Then, correct the information that is not true for you.

1. I drink cola for breakfast.

   <u>I don't drink cola for breakfast. I drink milk.</u>

2. I go to work every Sunday.

   _____

3. My teacher gives a test every day.

   _____

4. I go to school in the afternoon.

   _____

5. I take a long vacation every winter.

   _____

C. There is <u>one</u> mistake in each sentence. Correct the mistakes.

1. He <u>take</u> the bus to school.

2. She <u>don't drink</u> coffee in the evening.

3. They <u>eat out never</u> on Monday evenings.

4. My friends and I always <u>goes</u> to the movies on Saturday nights.

5. I usually work from 7:00 A.M. <u>at</u> 3:00 P.M.

Grammar Summary

▶ **1. Simple present tense** Use the simple present tense to talk about everyday actions. These actions happen every day, every weekend, every year, etc.

▶ **2. Statements**

I **work** from Monday to Friday.

We **study** on Tuesday and Thursday.

You **get** up early.

They **drive** to work every day.

He **works** from Monday to Friday.

She **studies** on Tuesday and Thursday.

The train **arrives** on time.

▶ **3. Negatives**

I **do not work** on Saturday.

We **do not study** on Wednesday.

You **do not get** up early.

They **do not drive** in the winter.

He **does not work** on Saturday.

She **does not study** on Wednesday.

The train **does not stop** here.

I **don't work** on Saturday.

We **don't study** on Wednesday.

You **don't get** up early.

They **don't drive** in the winter.

He **doesn't work** on Saturday.

She **doesn't study** on Wednesday.

The train **doesn't stop** here.

▶ **4. Time expressions and *How often . . . ?***

Put these time expressions at the end of the sentence.

How often do you work overtime?

How often do you take the bus?

How often do you go on vacation?

How often does she go to the gym?

I work overtime **once a month.**

I take the bus **every morning.**

We go on a vacation **every summer.**

She goes to the gym **three times a week.**

▶ **5. Adverbs of frequency**

Adverbs of frequency come <u>before</u> all verbs except the verb *to be*.

I **always** go to school.

I **usually** speak English in class.

I **sometimes** arrive early.

I **never** eat breakfast.

Adverbs of frequency come <u>after</u> the verb *to be*.

I am **always** on time.

I am **usually** quiet.

I am **sometimes** late for work.

I am **never** at home in the afternoon.

7 Airport Jobs

Dictionary: Jobs at the Airport

 A. Listen and repeat.

pilot	caterer	baggage handler
parking lot attendant	flight attendant	air traffic controller
cabin cleaner	ticket agent	aircraft mechanic
security screener	skycap	electric cart driver

B. Match the pictures and the airport jobs from the box.

1. _____

2. _____

3. _____

4. _____

5. _____

6. _____

7. _____

8. _____

9. _____

C. Complete.

1. A pilot ____flies____ a plane.

2. A baggage handler _____ luggage on the plane.

3. A security screener _____ passengers and their luggage.

4. An aircraft mechanic _____ the planes.

5. An electric cart driver _____ people who can't walk far.

6. A flight attendant _____ beverages and meals on a flight.

7. A parking lot attendant _____ parking fees from drivers.

8. A caterer _____ meals for flights.

9. A ticket agent _____ tickets.

10. An air traffic controller _____ planes in and out of the airport.

repairs
helps
✓ flies
collects
guides
puts
sells
checks
serves
prepares

D. *Who* questions. Answer these questions about airport jobs.

Who flies a plane?
A pilot does.
Pilots do.

Who repairs the planes?
An aircraft mechanic does.
Aircraft mechanics do.

1. Who wears a uniform?

2. Who uses a computer?

3. Who speaks English at work?

4. Who stands all day?

5. Who works outside?

6. Who has an interesting job?

7. Who has a boring job?

8. Who has a dangerous job?

9. Who has a stressful job?

10. Who has a high-paying job?

Write the opposites.

interesting _____

safe _____

high-paying _____

relaxing _____

Active Grammar: Present Tense Questions

 A. Listen and complete the information about Alberto's job.

Airport: <u>Atlanta Airport</u>

Job: _____

Days: _____

Hours: _____

Overtime: Yes   No

Uniform: Yes   No

B. Circle Alberto's answers. Then, write three more questions and answers.

1. Do you work at JFK Airport?   Yes, I do.   No, I don't.

2. Do you work at Atlanta Airport?   Yes, I do.   No, I don't.

3. Are you a pilot?   Yes, I am.   No, I'm not.

4. Do you work on Monday?   Yes, I do.   No, I don't.

5. Do you work on weekends?   Yes, I do.   No, I don't.

6. Do _____?   _____

7. _____?   _____

8. _____?   _____

C. Match. Then, read the conversation with a partner.

1. Where do you work?   I work from Wednesday to Sunday.

2. What do you do?   Yes, I put in a lot of overtime.

3. What's your schedule?   I work at Atlanta Airport.

4. Do you work overtime?   Yes, I do.

5. Do you wear a uniform?   I'm a mechanic.

6. Do you like your job?   Yes. I wear a blue uniform.

D. Read.

Ellen is a flight attendant. She works for Dove Airlines. She works at the Denver Airport. She makes passengers comfortable. She serves beverages and meals on the plane. She gives safety instructions. Ellen usually works from Monday to Thursday. Her schedule is from 7:00 A.M. to 4:00 P.M. But there are often delays, so sometimes she works from 7:00 A.M. to 7:00 P.M. She usually flies from Denver to Seattle. Ellen has a stressful job, but she likes her job a lot.

E. Circle. Then, write three more questions and answers.

1. Does Ellen work at Denver Airport?   Yes, she does.   No, she doesn't.

2. Is she a pilot?   Yes, she is.   No, she isn't.

3. Does she work for Universal Airlines?   Yes, she does.   No, she doesn't.

4. Does she work on the weekends?   Yes, she does.   No, she doesn't.

5. Does she fly from Denver to Miami?   Yes, she does.   No, she doesn't.

6. Does _____? _____

7. _____? _____

8. _____? _____

F. Listen and complete. Then, answer the questions.

1. Where _____does_____ Ellen _____?

2. What _____ she _____?

3. What airline _____ for?

4. What _____ her schedule?

5. _____ on weekends?

6. What route _____?

7. _____ her job?

G. Circle.

A: What **do / does** your sister **do / does**?

B: She's an air traffic controller.

A: Where **do / does** she **work / works**?

B: She **work / works** at Logan Airport.

A: What airline **do / does** she **work / works** for?

B: She doesn't work for an airline. She **work / works** for the airport.

H. Complete this conversation.

A: Where _____does_____ your brother _____work_____?

B: He works at Logan Airport.

A: What _____ he _____?

B: He's a skycap.

A: _____ he wear a uniform?

B: Yes, he does.

A: Which airline _____ he _____ for?

B: He works for World Airlines.

A: How much _____ he _____ an hour?

B: He makes $8 an hour plus tips.

I. Ask and answer questions about these employees.

1.

2.

3.

4.

Looking at the Classified Ads

A. Match.

a. FT — full time — experience

b. exp — part time

c. pref — full time

d. PT — department

e. dept — preferred

B. Read the classified ads. Then, answer the questions.

MANICURIST—licensed, exp with nail art. PT in busy salon. Must be available Sat. Apply in person. 378 Summit Avenue, Madison.

ROOFER—Residential work. Start immediately. Will train. Must have valid driver's license. Good pay. Call Dave 555-8076.

BAGGAGE HANDLER—FT position. Evening hours. Must work weekends. Apply in person. Personnel Dept., Atlanta Airport.

AUTO BODY REPAIR PERSON — Exp in taping, sanding, painting, and light body work. Small shop. Medical benefits and two weeks vacation. No weekends. Call George 555-8125.

1. What is the job?

2. Is it part time or full time?

3. Is experience required?

4. Do you need a car?

5. Do you need a special license?

6. Do you need to speak English well?

7. Do you need to work weekends?

8. Does the job offer benefits?

9. Who do you call or see about this job?

C. Classified advertisements.
Look in the classified advertisement section of your local newspaper. Cut out or copy two ads for jobs that you would like. Talk about the advertisements in your class.

☀ Talking About Salary and Benefits

A. Read.

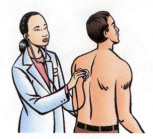

1. I have medical benefits.

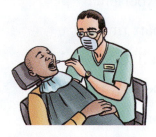

2. I have a dental plan.

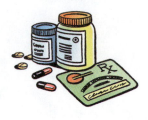

3. I have a prescription plan.

4. I have five sick days.

5. I have two weeks' vacation.

6. I have a retirement plan.

B. Complete about your benefits.

1. I **have / don't have** medical benefits.

2. I **have / don't have** a dental plan.

3. I **have / don't have** a prescription plan.

4. I have _____ sick days.

5. I have _____ weeks' vacation.

6. I also have _____.

Culture Note

Many companies pay overtime. Sometimes the overtime pay is two or three dollars more per hour. In some companies, overtime pay is time and a half. For example, if your salary is $10 an hour, overtime pay is $15 an hour.

Many companies pay double time for work on national holidays. What is your company's policy for overtime and holiday pay?

C. Listen and write the salary and benefits.

Employee	Salary	Overtime	Medical benefits	Dental plan	Sick days	Vacation
Karina	$8	$10	After 6 months		3	1 week
Mohamed						
Li-Ping						
Juan						

D. Ask and answer questions about the chart above.

1. What is _____'s salary?

2. How much is his/her overtime pay?

3. Does she have medical benefits / a dental plan / a prescription plan?

4. How many sick days does he/she have?

5. How many weeks' vacation does he/she get?

Working Together: Student to Student

A. STUDENT A: Ask your partner about Lena's job.

STUDENT B: Turn to page 100.

Job: <u>Ticket agent</u>

Airport: _____

Days: _____

Hours: _____

Salary: _____

Medical benefits: Yes   No

Dental plan: Yes   No

Sick days: _____ days

Vacation: _____ weeks

What does Lena do?
Where does she work?
What days does she work?
What's her schedule?
What's her salary?
Does she have _____ ?

Working Together: Student to Student

B. STUDENT B: Answer your partner's questions about Lena's job.

Job: Ticket agent

Airport: San Jose Airport

Days: Tuesday to Saturday

Hours: 6:00 A.M. to 2:00 P.M.

Salary: $600 a week

Medical benefits: (Yes)   No

Dental plan: Yes   (No)

Sick days: __7__ days

Vacation: __2__ weeks

Culture Note

In the United States, people consider it impolite to ask their friends or co-workers about their salaries.

C. Interview. Sit in a group of three students. Ask your partners about their jobs or the jobs they would like to have.

Questions	Student 1	Student 2
Where do you work?		
What do you do?		
How many days a week do you work?		
What hours do you work?		
Do you ever work overtime?		
Do you speak English at work?		
Do _____ a uniform?		
Do _____ ?		
_____ ?		

C. Work facts. These statements are true about work in the United States. Check the statements that are true about your country. Sit in a group and discuss your responses.

1. ☐ Full-time work is between 35 and 40 hours a week.

2. ☐ Most people drive to work.

3. ☐ There is a minimum wage.

4. ☐ Most full-time workers receive medical benefits.

5. ☐ Many high school students have part-time jobs.

6. ☐ 75% of women with children work outside the home.

7. ☐ Men and women sometimes receive the same salary for the same work.

8. ☐ Most service workers wear uniforms.

9. ☐ The standard retirement age is 67.

10. ☐ Most companies offer retirement plans.

D. Pronunciation: *Does he / Does she.*

Listen and repeat.

1. **a.** Does he work at the airport? **b.** Does she work at the airport?

2. **a.** Does he like his job? **b.** Does she like her job?

3. **a.** Does he wear a uniform? **b.** Does she wear a uniform?

Listen and complete.

1. Does _____ work full time?

2. Does _____ work on weekends?

3. Does _____ use a computer at work?

4. Does _____ speak English at work?

5. Does _____ need a driver's license?

6. Does _____ get good benefits?

7. Does _____ have a dental plan?

Practice the sentences above with a partner.

The Big Picture: The Interview

A. Listen. Mr. Chan is in the personnel office of a major airport. He is applying for a position as an electric cart driver.

B. Answer.

> Yes, he does.
> No, he doesn't.

1. Does Mr. Chan work at the airport now? _____Yes, he does._____

2. Does he drive an electric cart? _____

3. Does he make $8 an hour? _____

4. Does he have any violations on his license? _____

5. Does he have a good letter of reference? _____

6. Does he have experience with elderly people? _____

7. Does he have medical benefits now? _____

8. Does he have a dental plan now? _____

9. Does he speak English well? _____

10. Does he have the new job? _____

C. Complete with the interview vocabulary.

position	recommendation	available
personnel	✓interview	benefits
applicants	promotion	experience

Mr. Chan is on an _____interview_____ with Ms. Ross, the director of
_____. He is applying for a _____ as an electric cart
driver. This job would be a _____ for him because the salary is
higher and the job has more responsibility. Mr. Chan knows he has a good
chance to get the job. He has a good letter of _____ from his
supervisor. He has _____ with people in wheelchairs. He is
_____ to work any hours. Mr. Chan would like this job because the
salary is higher and it offers more _____ than his current job. Ms.
Ross is going to interview two more _____. After that, she will call
Mr. Chan.

D. Complete these questions about Mr. Chan.

1. Where __does he work_____? At the airport.

2. What _____? He's a parking lot attendant.

3. Why _____? Because the salary is higher.

4. What benefits _____? He receives medical benefits.

5. How much vacation _____? Two weeks.

E. Interview. Sit with a partner. Write a job interview. One student is the personnel director and the other student is the applicant. Use these questions to help you.

1. What do you do now? What are your responsibilities?

2. Why do you want this job?

3. Do you have any experience? Do you have a license or special training?

4. Can you _____?

Reading: A Job Posting

A. Before You Read.

Where can you find job postings?

WINGS AIRLINES

Position title: Ramp agent

Duties:

- Load and unload baggage
- Direct aircraft into the ramp area
- Fuel planes

Qualifications:

- At least 18 years old
- HS diploma or GED
- Driver's license and clean driving record
- Able to lift 70 pounds repetitively

- Very good physical condition
- Able to read and write English
- Available to work all shifts and weekends
- Authorized to work in the United States

Pay:

- First year: $9.00 an hour   Second year: $11.00 an hour

Benefits:

- Medical insurance for employee
- Vacation: Years 1 to 3: two weeks
             Years 4 to 6: three weeks

- Three personal days
- Free flights on a space-available basis

Call for an interview: 555-7878

Bring to your interview: Your driver's license, resume, two letters of reference, copy of high school diploma

---

B. Circle *True* or *False*.

1. A ramp agent loads and unloads baggage.   (True)   False

2. A ramp agent must have a special driver's license.   True   False

3. A ramp agent has a heavy job.   True   False

4. A ramp agent needs to speak English.   True   False

5. A ramp agent earns $11 an hour the first year.   True   False

6. A ramp agent receives medical insurance.   True   False

7. A ramp agent gets three weeks of vacation the second year.   True   False

8. An applicant must bring a resume to the interview.   True   False

9. A ramp agent can always fly for free.   True   False

Writing Our Stories: My Job

A. Read.

My name is Nelson. I'm a security screener at New Orleans Airport. I sit at the scanner. I check people when they walk through the gate. If there is a problem, I call my supervisor. I work full time. My schedule is always different. I work different days each week. I usually work in the afternoon and in the evening. I don't have good medical benefits. I have five sick days and two weeks' vacation. I like my job at the airport. It is busy and exciting. There are many jobs here. I hope to get a promotion in the future.

B. Write. Complete this information about your job. Write a few more sentences about your work.

I am a _____ at _____.
             position   company

I _____ and _____.
   responsibility   responsibility

I work _____. I work from _____ to _____,
     full time / part time   day   day

from _____ to _____. I _____
      time   time   have / don't have

good job benefits. I have _____
                                benefits

_____

_____

_____

_____

Writing Note

Use a colon when you write the time: 6:00, 4:30.

You can use capital or lowercase letters for A.M. and P.M.: 6:00 A.M. or 6:00 a.m.

Practicing on Your Own

A. Complete with *Do* or *Does*. Write the short answer.

1. ____Do____ pilots travel a lot?   Yes, they do.

2. _____ an air traffic controller have a stressful jobs?   _____

3. _____ many flight attendants speak two languages?   _____

4. _____ a baggage handler lift heavy bags and boxes?   _____

5. _____ a personnel director interview job applicants?   _____

6. _____ ticket agents stand all day?   _____

7. _____ passengers often wait many hours in airports?   _____

8. _____ a passenger need ID in an airport?   _____

9. _____ all airport employees speak English?   _____

10. _____ an aircraft mechanic need special training?   _____

B. Read this story. Then, complete the questions.

Jeff Miller is a pilot. He lives in Boston and works at Logan Airport. He flies international routes, usually from Boston to London. He works four days a week. On Monday, he flies from Boston to London. He stays overnight in London. Then, he flies back on Tuesday. He has two days off, and then he repeats this schedule on Friday and Saturday. Jeff earns about $150,000 a year and he has excellent benefits. He loves to fly, and he travels all over the world. He doesn't like the headaches at the airport. Air traffic is always heavy, and there are often long delays. His days are often 10 to 12 hours long.

1. What _does Jeff Miller do_____? He's a pilot.

2. Where _____? At Logan Airport.

3. What route _____? From Boston to London.

4. How many days _____? Four.

5. How much _____? $150,000 a year.

6. _____? All over the world.

7. _____? Yes, he does.

8. _____? No, he doesn't.

Looking at Numbers: Salaries

A. Figure out the salaries.

1. Kathy works part time. She makes $8 an hour. She works 20 hours a week. What is her salary?

2. Ivan works 25 hours a week. His earns $11 an hour. What is his salary?

3. Vinh works full time, 40 hours a week. His salary is $15 an hour. What is his weekly salary?

4. Dorota works full time. She makes $10 an hour. She makes $14 an hour overtime. She usually works 50 hours a week. What is her salary?

5. Roya likes to work holidays because she makes double time. She makes $14 an hour. If she works eight hours on Thanksgiving, what is her pay for that day?

6. Mustafa works 40 hours a week, plus eight hours on Sunday. His salary is $12 an hour plus time and a half for Sunday. What is his weekly salary?

Grammar Summary

▶ **1. *Yes/No* questions**

Do I work?	Yes, you do.	No, you don't.
Do you work?	Yes, I do.	No, I don't.
Do we work?	Yes, you do.	No, you don't.
Do they work?	Yes, they do.	No, they don't.
Does he work?	Yes, he does.	No, he doesn't.
Does she work?	Yes, she does.	No, she doesn't.
Does it work?	Yes, it does.	No, it doesn't.

▶ **2. *Wh-* questions**

Where do I work?	**Where** does he work?
When do you work?	**When** does she work?
What hours do we work?	**Why** does it work?
What days do they work?	

▶ **3. *Who* questions (*Who* as subject)**

Who works full time?   Alberto does.   Alberto and Ela do.

8 A College Campus

Dictionary: The Campus

A. Listen and repeat.

benches	mailbox	lights
garbage cans	bus stop	statue
dogs	students	security guards
cars	pay telephone	security booth
flag	parking lot	

B. Label each person, place, or thing on the campus.

Active Grammar: *There is/There are*

A. Listen and complete with *is* or *are* and a quantity expression.

a	a few	several	some	a lot of	many	any

1. There ____are____ ____a few____ benches outside.

2. There _____ _____ students outside the building.

3. There _____ _____ statue in front of the building.

4. There _____ _____ garbage cans outside.

5. There _____ _____ pay telephone next to the building.

6. There _____ _____ bus at the bus stop.

7. There _____ _____ cars in the parking lot.

8. There _____ _____ students at the bus stop.

> **a few**   a small number, for example, three or four
>
> **several**   more than a few, for example, five, or six, or seven

B. Write seven sentences about your classroom. Do not use a number. Use a quantity expression.

C. *How many* questions. Ask and answer questions about the picture on page 108.

How many flags are there?	There is one.
How many cars are in the parking lot?	There are a lot.
How many trees are next to the building?	There aren't any.

1. How many students are outside the building?

2. How many dogs are outside?

3. How many mailboxes are next to the building?

4. How many cars are in front of the building?

5. How many windows are in the building?

6. How many security guards _____?

7. How many flags _____?

8. How many _____?

D. *Is there . . . ? / Are there . . . ?* Answer these questions about your classroom or your building.

> **Is there a television in your classroom?**
> **Yes, there is.**
> **No, there isn't.**

> **Are there any maps on the walls?**
> **Yes, there are.**
> **No, there aren't.**

1. Is there a television in your classroom?
2. Are there any computers in your classroom?
3. Is there a world map in your classroom?
4. Is there a map of the United States in your classroom?
5. Is there a pencil sharpener in your classroom?
6. Are there any restrooms on your floor?
7. Are there any escalators in your building?
8. Is there an elevator in your building?
9. Are there any computer labs in your building?
10. Are there any vending machines in your building?

 E. With a partner, write five more questions about your classroom or your building. Then, combine groups and ask other students your questions.

 F. Polite questions. Read the situations. Ask questions with *Is there* or *Are there.*

> **You need to make a telephone call.**
> **Is there a public telephone in this building?**

1. You want to mail a letter.
2. You need to wash your hands.
3. You want to sharpen your pencil.
4. You would like a drink of water.
5. You need to make a copy of a paper.
6. You broke your foot and you can't walk up the stairs.
7. You would like a can of soda.
8. You would like something to eat.

G. College information. Complete these questions.

1. There are many colleges in the United States.

   A: How many <u>colleges are there in the United States</u>?

   B: There are more than 4,000 colleges in the United States.

2. There are many four-year colleges in the United States.

   A: How many _____?

   B: There are about 2,300 four-year colleges in the United States.

3. There are many two-year colleges in the United States.

   A: How many _____?

   B: There are more than 1,700 two-year colleges in the United States.

4. There are many colleges in California.

   A: How many _____?

   B: There are about 400 colleges in California.

5. There are not many colleges in Alaska.

   A: How many _____?

   B: There are eight colleges in Alaska.

6. There are many students in college in the United States.

   A: How many _____?

   B: There are about 15 million students in college.

7. There are many women in college in the United States.

   A: How many _____?

   B: There are about 8,500,000 women in college.

College Information

How many colleges are there in your state?
Name four colleges in your state.
Which college is the closest to your home?
Is it a two-year college or a four-year college?

H. Pronunciation: *there, they*. Listen and repeat.

1.	They are here.	5.	They are in class.
2.	There are four here.	6.	There are many students in class.
3.	They aren't here.	7.	They aren't in class.
4.	There aren't any here.	8.	There aren't any students in class.

 I. Listen and complete these sentences.

1. _____ _____ many cars on campus.

2. _____ _____ in the parking lot.

3. _____ _____ any buses.

4. _____ _____ on the bus.

5. _____ _____ any students in the cafeteria.

6. _____ _____ in class.

7. _____ _____ many students in the gym.

8. _____ _____ in the pool.

 Practice the sentences above with a partner.

J. (Circle.)

1. **There / They** are four students walking into the building. **They / There** are early.

2. **There / It** is a bus stop on campus. **There / They** aren't any students waiting for the bus. **There / They** are in class.

3. **There / It** is a mailbox in front of the building. **There / It** is full.

4. **There / They** are several lights in the parking lot. **There / They** aren't on now because it's daytime. **There / They** are only on at night.

5. **There / They** are many cars in the parking lot. **There / They** are not students' cars because this is a faculty parking lot. **There / They** are four parking lots for students.

6. **There / It** is a pay telephone booth next to the building. **There / It** is empty.

A. STUDENT A: Listen to Student B. Write each sentence next to the correct picture.

STUDENT B: Turn to page 114. Read the eight sentences to your partner.

1. _____
   _____

2. _____
   _____

1. _____
   _____

2. _____
   _____

1. _____
   _____

2. _____
   _____

1. _____
   _____

2. _____
   _____

When you finish, Student A will turn to page 114. Student B will turn back to this page and listen to eight new sentences. Write each sentence next to the correct picture.

B. Read these sentences to your partner.

STUDENT B

a. There are two dictionaries on this desk.

b. There are two erasers on this desk.

c. There is one pencil on this desk.

d. There's a can of soda on this desk.

e. There are several pencils on this desk.

f. There isn't any paper on this desk.

g. There is a pair of glasses on this desk.

h. There are a few books on this desk.

STUDENT A

a. There are two pencils on this desk.

b. There aren't any pencils on this desk.

c. There aren't any dictionaries on this desk.

d. There isn't any coffee on this desk.

e. There are several keys on this desk.

f. There's a lot of paper on this desk.

g. There is a piece of paper on this desk.

h. There is a pack of gum on this desk.

C. Our classroom. Complete these sentences about your class and your school.

1. There _____ _____ students in my class.

2. There _____ _____ man / men.

3. There _____ _____ woman / women.

4. There _____ _____ student(s) from Mexico.

5. There _____ _____ student(s) from Japan.

6. There _____ _____ student(s) from _____.

7. There _____ _____ teenager(s)

8. There _____ _____ teacher.

9. There _____ _____ married students.

10. There _____ _____ single students.

11. There _____ _____ maps in our classroom.

12. There _____ _____ computers in our classroom.

13. There _____ _____ desks in our classroom.

14. There _____ _____ clock(s) in our classroom.

15. There _____ _____ electrical outlets in our classroom.

D. A blueprint. Work in groups of three or four students. Go to different rooms or areas in your school building: for example, the cafeteria, library, lobby, main floor, lounge, etc. Draw a detailed blueprint of the area. Only include large items in your drawing, such as desks, tables, bookshelves, and other furniture. Write 10 sentences about the room. Come back to class, and draw your blueprint on the chalkboard or a large piece of paper. Describe the room or area to your classmates.

E. *How many* questions. Ask the question for each pair of words. Match each question with the correct number.

How many days are there in a week?
There are seven (7).

9

50

7

26

days / week?

days / year?

weeks / year?

9

players / baseball team?

365

states / the United States?

52

planets / solar system?

letters / alphabet?

12

3

ounces / pound?

12

inches / foot?

13

4

quarts / gallon?

3

items / dozen?

6

4

countries / North America?

16

stripes / American flag?

sides / triangle?

sides / cube?

sides / square?

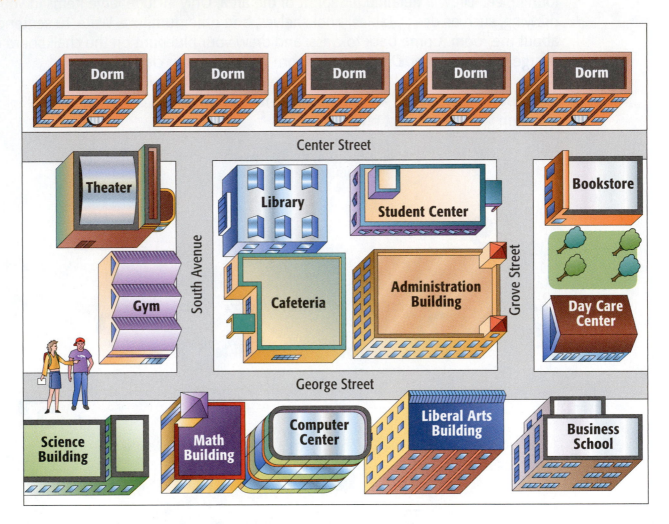

 A. Listen and write the symbol for each location on the correct location on the map above.

1. tennis courts

2. ATM machine

3. pay telephones

4. parking lot

5. mailbox

6. bus stop

B. Answer these questions about the campus.

1. Are there any tennis courts on campus?

   There are four tennis courts in back of the gym.

2. Are there any pay telephones on campus?

   _____

3. Are there any mailboxes on campus?

   _____

4. Are there any ATM machines on campus?

   _____

5. Is there a bus stop on campus?

   _____

C. Complete with *it*, *they*, or *there*.

1. *There* _____ are five dormitories on campus. *They* _____ are on Center Street.

2. _____ is a day care center on campus. _____ is on the corner of George Street and Grove Street.

3. _____ is a large library. _____ has books on every subject.

4. _____ are many parking lots for students, but _____ are usually full.

5. _____ are four tennis courts in back of the gym. _____ are four more in back of the liberal arts building.

6. _____ are only two pay phones on campus. Students don't need pay phones because _____ have cell phones.

7. _____ is an active theater on campus. _____ are music and art performances every week. _____ are free movies every Monday night.

D. Write a paragraph about this campus. Describe the location of the buildings and the facilities.

Reading: College 101

A. Before You Read.

What are some of your class rules?

   In high school, students learn how to study. Students have classes every period and follow a regular schedule. In college, students have free periods during the day. Their schedules may be different each day. In college, students are adults. They are responsible for their schedules and studying. What are some of the expectations of college students?

1. Attend the first day of class. Get all first day notes, which may include a list of assignments, test information, syllabus, calendar, class rules, and so on.

2. Get to class on time. Turn your cell phones and beepers off! Bring your books with you. Sharpen your pencil <u>before</u> class.

3. Attend your classes regularly. You are responsible for the information in your books, assignments, and class notes.

4. Find one or two partners the first week or two of class. Study together. Share your notes. If one of you is absent, get the homework from your partner.

5. Look at the professor from time to time. This shows that you are listening. When you speak, look directly at your teacher.

6. Ask questions. Participate in class discussions.

7. Do your homework. Hand in all papers and reports on time.

8. Find the tutoring center. Most colleges have study centers with tutors, computer programs, and writing help.

B. Which information is true about colleges in the United States? Circle *T* or *F.*

1. Your teacher will understand if you hand in a paper late.   T   F

2. You should never look directly in your teacher's eyes.   T   F

3. Always do your homework alone. Do not work with another student.   T   F

4. Students are only responsible for the information in the book.   T   F

5. College teachers often hand out important papers during the first class.   T   F

6. If you ask a question, the teacher will think you are not studying.   T   F

7. You are alone at college. You must succeed by yourself.   T   F

C. Which expectations are the same in your native country? Which are different?

Writing Our Stories: My School

A. Read.

I attend UCSD, the University of California San Diego. The campus is very big. There are many buildings. There are dormitories, classroom buildings, libraries, theaters, and cafeterias. There is an indoor pool and an outdoor pool.

I am a student at the English Language Program. There are about 1,000 students in English classes during the year. Our program is in a small group of buildings. There are about twenty classrooms and two computer labs. In the center, there is a large patio. The weather in San Diego is warm and sunny all year, so we are often outside. We sit on the patio and talk and study and work in small groups. There is only one problem with our campus. It is too big! It is a fifteen-minute walk from here to the pool.

B. Check (✓) some of the buildings or facilities at your school.

☐ library   ☐ cafeteria

☐ study center   ☐ gym

☐ day care center   ☐ parking lot

☐ student center   ☐ dormitory

☐ bookstore

☐ computer center

☐ theater

☐ _____

> ## Writing Note
> Use a comma in a list of people, places, or things: There are dormitories, classroom buildings, libraries, theaters, and cafeterias.

C. In your notebook, describe your school.

A. Circle the correct words in these questions and answers.

1. **A:** **Is / Are** there any students from China in your class?

   B: Yes, there **is / are** five students from China. **They / There** are from Beijing.

2. **A:** Is there **an / any** elevator in this building?

   B: Yes, **there / it** is. **There / It** is at the end of the hall.

3. **A:** **Is / Are** there a ladies room on this floor?

   B: No, there **isn't / aren't**. **There / It** is one on the second floor.

4. **A:** Are there any vending **machine / machines** on this floor?

   B: Yes, **they / there** are. **There / They** are in the student lounge.

5. **A:** Is there a copy **machine / machines** for student use?

   B: Yes, **there / it** is one in the library. It costs ten cents a copy.

6. **A:** Are there many **computer / computers** in the library?

   B: Yes, there are **one / a lot of** computers in the library.

7. **A:** **Is / Are** there a fax machine in the library?

   B: No, there **isn't / aren't**. There is **a / some** fax machine in the student center.

B. Complete these questions about time. Write the answers.

1. How many seconds _____are_____ _____there_____ in a minute?
   There are 60 seconds in a minute.

2. How many minutes _____ _____ in an hour?
   _____

3. How many hours _____ _____ in a day?
   _____

4. How many months _____ _____ in a year?
   _____

5. How many days _____ _____ in a year?
   _____

6. How many years _____ _____ in decade?
   _____

Looking at Forms: Registration Form

A. Answer these questions about Adam's registration form.

Registration Form

Wojik	Adam	152 _ 15 _ 1515
Last name	First name	Student ID Number

Course / Number	Section	Credit Hours	Day	Time	Room
English 102	136	3	M-W	9:00	N317
Math 203	251	3	M-W	11:00	M305
Comp Sc. 210	204	4	T-R	10:00	T406
BIO 105	131	4	T-R	2:00	S112
Bio LAB 105	107	1	F	12:00	S102

Student Signature _____ Adam Wojik _____   Advisor's Signature _____ R. Dewey _____   Date _ 8/15 _

1. What classes is Adam taking?
2. What days does Adam's computer class meet? What time is the class?
3. What days does his math class meet? What time is the class? What's the room number?

Grammar Summary

▶ **1. There is/There are: Statements**

There	is	a	student computer desk	in the classroom.
	are	a few several a lot of	students computers desks	

▶ **2.**

Affirmative	Negative
There **is a** computer in the room.	There **isn't a** computer in the room. There **is no** computer in the room.
There **are some** computers in the room.	There **aren't any** computers in the room. There **are no** computers in the room.

▶ **3. How many questions**

How many students are there in the classroom?	There are 20.
How many clocks are there in the classroom?	There is one.
How many computers are there in the classroom?	There aren't any.

9 At Work

 Dictionary: Occupations

 A. Listen and repeat.

assembler	custodian	machine operator
cable installer	electrician	nurse's aide
construction worker	high-lo driver	packer
cook	landscaper / gardener	painter

B. Label the jobs.

1. _____

2. _____

3. _____

4. _____

5. _____

6. _____

7. _____

8. _____

9. _____

10. _____

11. _____

12. _____

C. Listen and repeat.

apron	flashlight	hammer	leaf blower	mower	shovel
boots	forklift	hard hat	mask	paintbrush	tape
earplugs	gloves	I.D. badge	mixer	safety glasses	tool belt
earphones	hairnet	name tag	mop	screwdriver	work boots

D. Match each tool with the correct picture.

__e__ **1.** flashlight

____ **2.** forklift

____ **3.** hammer

____ **4.** tape

____ **5.** mixer

____ **6.** mop

____ **7.** mower

____ **8.** shovel

____ **9.** leaf blower

____ **10.** tool belt

____ **11.** hairnet

____ **12.** name tag / I.D. badge

a.

b.

c.

d.

e.

f.

g.

h.

i.

j.

k.

l.

Active Grammar: Present Continuous

A. Match the equipment with the job. You can use a tool more than once.

1. gardener
2. cable installer
4. machine operator
5. packer
6. construction worker
7. custodian
8. painter
9. nurse's aide
10. electrician

a. tape
b. latex gloves
c. work boots
d. shovel
e. safety glasses
f. paintbrush
g. screwdriver
h. mop
i. flashlight

B. Complete about the equipment.

clothes	ears	eyes	feet	hands	head	lungs

1. An apron protects your _clothes_____.

2. Boots protect your _____.

3. Earplugs and earphones protect your
   _____.

4. A hard hat protects your _____.

5. A mask protects your _____.

6. Safety glasses protect your _____.

7. Gloves protect your _____.

C. *Who* questions. Ask and answer.

assembler
cable installer
cook
construction worker
custodian
electrician
high-lo driver
landscaper
machine operator
nurse's aide
packer
painter

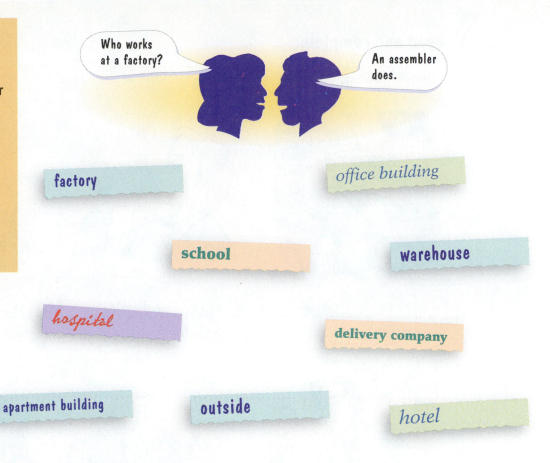

Who works at a factory?

An assembler does.

factory

office building

school

warehouse

hospital

delivery company

apartment building

outside

hotel

 D. Complete with a partner.

1. An electrician uses a <u>screwdriver</u>.

2. A construction worker uses a _____.

3. A landscaper uses a _____.

4. A(n) _____ uses earplugs.

5. A(n) _____ uses a hammer.

6. A(n) _____ wears work boots.

7. A(n) _____ wears an apron.

8. At my job, I use _____ and _____.

9. At my job, I wear _____ and _____.

A. Read and complete.

| drink | eat | go | listen to | look at | read | sit | take |

1. He is _____taking_____ a break.

2. He is _____drinking_____ a soda.

3. He is _____ some chips.

4. He is _____ to music.

5. He is _____ a magazine.

6. He is _____ on the couch.

7. She is _____ to work.

8. She is _____ her schedule.

9. She is _____ a newspaper.

greet	install	load	open	pack	talk	wash	wear

10. She is ——————— to co-workers.

11. She is ——————— her co-workers.

12. She is ——————— a uniform.

13. They are ———————.

14. They are ——————— cables.

15. They are ——————— the truck.

16. They are ——————— boxes.

17. They are ——————— boxes.

18. They are ——————— the boxes onto the truck.

B. Read and complete.

Present Continuous		
I	am	
You We They	are	working.
He She It	is	

clean   drive   cut   pack

Picture 1

1. What's she doing?

She ___is___ ___cleaning___ the floor.

2. What's she wearing?

She ___is___ ___wearing___ a uniform.

Picture 2

1. What's he doing?

He _____ _____ a tree.

2. What's he wearing?

He _____ _____ a hat

and _____.

Picture 3

1. What's she doing?

She _____ _____ a high-lo.

2. What's she wearing?

She _____ _____ a hard hat.

Picture 4

1. What are they doing?

They _____ _____ boxes.

2. What are they wearing?

They _____

_____.

In the Break Room

A. Look at the picture. It's break time. What are the employees doing?
Talk about the picture.

buy	eat	get	read	sit	stand	talk	walk	watch

B. Complete the sentences.

1. Luis and Gloria _____*are sitting*_____ on the couch.

2. They _____ TV.

3. Victor _____ a cup of water.

4. Vladimir _____ some candy.

5. Marie _____ to Mei-Lin.

6. They _____ lunch.

7. Joseph _____ in the break room.

8. He _____ a newspaper.

9. Anna and Louise _____ around the parking lot.

10. They _____ about babies.

 Negatives

I	am not	
He She It	is not	working.
We You They	are not	

A. Circle the verbs that are true for you.

1. I **am wearing / am not wearing** a uniform.

2. I **am wearing / am not wearing** glasses.

3. I **am wearing / am not wearing** a name tag.

4. I **am wearing / am not wearing** work boots.

5. I **am using / am not using** a pencil.

6. I **am using / am not using** a computer.

7. I **am drinking / am not drinking** a cup of tea.

 Read your sentences to a partner.

 B. Pronunciation: *I'm working.* Listen and repeat.

1. I'm working.

2. I'm driving.

3. I'm talking to my boss.

4. I'm sitting in class.

5. I'm eating dinner.

 C. I'm busy. Listen to the conversation. Then, practice the conversation with a partner. Use the excuses in Exercise B.

A: Hello?

B: Hi, this is _____ Roger _____.

A: Hi, _____ Roger _____. I can't talk to you now.

_____ I'm working _____. I'll call you back.

B: Okay, I'll talk to you later.

Working Together

A. What's wrong with this picture? Look at the pictures. Something is wrong with each picture. Talk about the pictures with a partner.

| carry | clean | sit | wear | push | pull |

Fred   Miguel   Michelle   Iris and Martha   Mr. Tanaka

Fred isn't wearing a hard hat and shoes.
He is wearing a straw hat and slippers.

B. Interview. Talk to a person who works in your school. Ask the person, *"What's your name?"*, *"What's your occupation?"*, and *"When do you work?"* Ask, *"Can I observe you?"* Then, observe the person for 5 to 10 minutes.

C. Complete the sentences about the person that you are observing.

1. _____ **is / isn't** speaking on the telephone.

2. _____ **is / isn't** standing.

3. **He / She   is / isn't** working behind a counter.

4. **He / She   is / isn't** working at a desk.

5. **He / She   is / isn't** wearing a uniform.

6. **He / She   is / isn't** using a computer.

7. **He / She   is / isn't** answering the telephone.

8. **He / She   is / isn't** handling money.

D. Write five more sentences about your observation.

The Big Picture: Inspection at the Factory

A. Look at the picture. Talk about the employees. What's happening at the factory?

Culture Note

OSHA (Occupational Safety and Health Administration) is a federal organization that tries to keep workers safe.

 B. Listen and write the names of the employees.

| Mr. Brooks | Victor | Carmen | Anna | Frank | Louise | Vladimir |

C. (Circle) the answers.

1. Is the factory busy?

   a. Yes, it is.   **b.** No, it isn't.   **c.** It's hot.

2. Why is Mr. DiMauro at the factory?

   a. He's an employee.   **b.** He's the inspector.   **c.** He's an assembler.

3. Who is smoking?

   a. Victor is.   **b.** Vladimir is.   **c.** Luis is.

4. Who is wearing a hairnet?

    a. Carmen is.   **b.** Gloria is.   **c.** Anna is.

5. Is Vladimir wearing work boots?

    a. Yes, he is.   **b.** No, he isn't.   **c.** No, she isn't.

6. Who isn't wearing safety glasses?

    a. Luis.   **b.** Carmen.   **c.** Joseph.

7. Who isn't wearing a hard hat?

    a. Joseph.   **b.** Victor.   **c.** Frank and Joseph.

8. Who is very tired?

    a. Gloria is.   **b.** Joseph is.   **c.** Louise is.

D. Complete. Some of the sentences are negative.

1. Victor _is smoking_____ .

2. Gloria _____ a hairnet.

3. Carmen _____ safety glasses.

4. Frank and Joseph _____ their hard hats.

5. Vladimir _____ sandals.

6. Louise _____ . She's very tired.

7. Gloria _____ gloves.

8. Joseph _____ the high-lo without his hard hat.

> drive
> ✓ smoke
> stand
> wear
> drive

E. Ask and answer the questions with a partner.

1. What is Vladimir wearing?

2. What is he carrying?

3. What is Luis wearing for safety?

4. Who isn't wearing a hairnet?

5. What is Joseph driving?

6. What aren't Frank and Joseph wearing?

7. What is Louise doing?

8. Is she sitting?

9. Is Mr. Brooks worried?

Reading: Holiday Deliveries

A. Before You Read.

1. What season is the busiest season for delivery companies?

2. How many delivery companies can you name?

3. Do you know someone who works for a delivery company?

It's fall, and delivery companies are busy. They are getting ready for the busy holiday season. Every year, in the fall, many delivery companies advertise for part-time positions. The companies need more employees for holiday deliveries. The companies are looking for more package handlers. Package handlers sort and load the many packages that customers want to send.

> **Package handlers**
> Part-time $8.50–$9.50
> 3½ – 5 hours per day
> No weekends
> 3 Shifts: 1:00/4:00/5:30
> Individual medical benefits
> Paid vacation

The largest delivery companies deliver packages in more than 200 countries and deliver more than 13.5 million packages a day. They deliver packages by air or on the ground by truck. The truck drivers wear uniforms that change according to the season. In the hot summer, the drivers may wear shorts.

Over a million people work for delivery companies, and there are many jobs available. Would you like to work for a delivery company?

B. Read and circle.

1. Delivery companies need more employees

    a. in the summer.　　b. in the winter.　　c. in the fall.　　d. in the spring.

2. Delivery companies need people to

    a. handle packages.　b. sell packages.　　c. help salesmen.　d. fly planes.

3. Delivery companies deliver packages

    a. by air.　　　　　　b. by sea.　　　　　c. by land.　　　　d. both a and c.

4. This classified ad is looking for people who can

    a. work in the morning.　　　　　c. work eight-hour shifts.
    b. work weekends.　　　　　　　d. work part time.

5. What benefits will the package handlers receive? (Circle two answers.)

    a. medical benefits　　　　　　c. prescription plan
    b. paid vacation　　　　　　　d. paid sick days

Writing Our Stories: Home Improvements

A. Look at the picture. Write a story about the people in the picture. What are their occupations? What are they wearing? What are they doing at the house?

build
deliver
fix
install
mow
paint
plant
repair
deck
garage
roof
tree

B. Write your story.

_____

_____

_____

_____

_____

_____

_____

_____

_____

_____

_____

Writing Note

Give your story a title. Put the title in the center of the top line. The words in the title begin with capital letters.

A. Look at the picture. Read and complete. Some of the sentences are negative.

The safety inspector is back at the factory. He is very happy with the changes.

cook	
drive	
follow	
sit	
wash	
wear	

1. Gloria and Marie _____ hairnets.

2. Gloria and Marie _____ lunch for the employees.

3. Vladimir _____ sandals. He _____ work boots.

4. Luis and Anna _____ safety glasses.

5. Louise _____ in a chair. She _____ standing.

6. Wilson _____ his hands.

7. Joseph _____ a hard hat.

8. Joseph _____ a high-lo.

9. All of the employees _____ safety rules.

In your notebook, write four more sentences about the picture.

Grammar Summary

▶ **1. Present continuous tense** Use the present continuous to talk about what's happening now.

▶ **2. Some present continuous time expressions**

now	right now	at the present time	at the moment

▶ **3. Statements**

I	**am** **am not**	**packing** boxes.
He She It	**is** **is not / isn't**	**taking** a break.
We You They	**are** **are not / aren't**	**wearing** a uniform.

▶ **4. Spelling**

Verb ending	**Spelling**

• Most verbs
  drink
  read
  study
	Add **-ing**.
	  drinking
	  reading
	  studying

• Verbs that end with **e**
  write
  take
	Drop the **e** and add **-ing**.
	  writing
	  taking

• One-syllable verbs that end with a
  consonant, vowel, consonant
  sit
  mop
	Double the final vowel
	and add **-ing**.
	  sitting
	  mopping

• Verbs that end with **x, y,** or **z**
  fix
  buy
	Do not double **x, y,** or **z**.
	  fixing
	  buying

10 Fast Food

Dictionary: Working at a Restaurant

A. Listen and repeat.

carry	eat	make	pay	serve	wear
cook	greet	order	pour	talk to	wipe

B. Complete.

1. The manager __is__
__greeting__ customers.

2. He _____
the table.

3. He _____
the employees.

4. They _____
coffee.

5. They _____
customers.

6. They _____
uniforms.

7. He _____
a sandwich.

8. He _____
the cashier.

9. He _____
a hamburger.

10. She _____
some coffee.

11. She _____
eggs.

12. She _____
her food.

C. Look at the pictures. Complete the sentences.

mop	prepare	wash	wipe

1. Jennifer _____ a table.

2. Nicholas and Nancy _____ donuts.

3. Kristina _____ pots.

4. Scott _____ the floor.

D. Complete.

cashier	cash register	counter	customers	in line

in line = on line

1. Penny and Ruth are standing at the _____.

2. They are _____ at the restaurant.

3. They are waiting _____.

4. Jane is a _____.

5. She is working at the _____.

Active Grammar: Present Continuous Questions — Yes/No Questions

A. Read and answer.

Yes, she is. No, she isn't.	Yes, he is. No, he isn't.	Yes, they are. No, they aren't.

1. **Is** Jane **working** today? _____ Yes, she is. _____

2. **Is** she **making** sandwiches? _____

3. **Is** Mr. Lopez **ordering** coffee? _____

4. **Is** he **ordering** a large coffee? _____

5. **Is** Nicholas **wiping** the counter? _____

6. **Are** customers **waiting** in line? _____

7. **Are** the customers **talking** to each other? _____

8. **Are** customers **eating** donuts? _____

B. Write five more questions about the picture. Ask and answer questions with a partner.

1. Is Nicholas _____?

2. Is Mr. Lopez _____?

3. Are Jane and Nicholas _____?

4. _____?

5. _____?

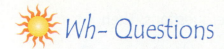

Wh- Questions

A. Listen and complete with the question words.

decaf — decaffeinated coffee
Decaffeinated coffee does not have caffeine.

1.	_____ are they eating?	They're eating breakfast.
2.	_____ is Mary eating?	She's eating eggs and a bagel.
3.	_____ are they having breakfast?	They're having breakfast at Coffee to Go.
4.	_____ is Vera drinking?	She's drinking orange juice.
5.	_____ donuts is Vera eating?	She's eating two donuts.
6.	_____ is drinking coffee?	Patricia is.
7.	_____ coffee is Patricia drinking?	She's drinking decaf coffee.
8.	_____ are they smiling?	Because they're enjoying breakfast.

B. Match each question with the correct answer.

1. Who is Mary eating with?   **a.** She's eating two donuts.
2. What is Scott doing?   **b.** Patricia is.
3. Who is eating a bagel?   **c.** She's eating with her friends.
4. Where are they working?   **d.** Because it is dirty.
5. Why is she wiping the table?   **e.** A sesame bagel.
6. How many donuts is Vera eating?   **f.** At Coffee to Go
7. What kind of bagel is she eating? **g.** He's mopping the floor.

C. ***Yes/No questions.*** Look at the picture. Complete the questions. Then, answer the questions with a partner.

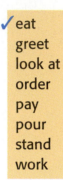

1. ___Is___ Jane _____eating_____ donuts?
2. _____ Nicholas _____ a customer?
3. _____ the customers _____ juice?
4. _____ Jane _____ at the cash register?
5. _____ Jane and Nicholas _____ hard?
6. _____ the student _____ the clock?
7. _____ Nicholas _____ tea?

✓ eat
greet
look at
order
pay
pour
stand
work

D. ***Wh-*** **questions.** Put the words in the questions in the correct order.

1. who / sitting / is / next to you / ?
2. who / writing / is / ?
3. your teacher / doing / is / what / ?
4. speaking / why / English / you / are / ?
5. what / you / doing / are / ?
6. working / with you / is / who / ?
7. studying / the students / are / where / ?
8. learning / who / English / is / ?

 Ask and answer the questions with a partner.

Stating Prices

 A. Pronunciation: Prices. Listen and repeat.

a.	$1.29	a dollar twenty-nine	or	one dollar and twenty-nine cents
b.	$3.50	three fifty	or	three dollars and fifty cents
c.	$4.16	four sixteen	or	four dollars and sixteen cents
d.	$6.99	six ninety-nine	or	six dollars and ninety-nine cents
e.	$10.25	ten twenty-five	or	ten dollars and twenty-five cents
f.	$12.05	twelve oh five	or	twelve dollars and five cents
g.	$14.30	fourteen thirty	or	fourteen dollars and thirty cents

Practice saying these prices with a partner.

a. $3.10	c. $5.50	e. $2.15	g. $17.47	i. $15.30
b. $11.05	d. $13.87	f. $6.75	h. $9.25	

Working Together: Student to Student

A. STUDENT A: Turn to page 144. Look at the menu.

STUDENT B: You both have menus with different prices missing. Ask and answer questions about the missing prices and fill in the menu.

Hamburger	**$1.49**	French fries	small	.99
Cheeseburger	1.79		large	1.39
Super Burger	2.99	Soft drink	small	
Chicken Sandwich			medium	
Fish Sandwich			large	1.39
Chicken Pieces	2.89	Coffee		
Salad bar		Apple pie		1.29

Working Together: Student to Student

B. STUDENT A: You both have menus with different prices missing. Ask and answer questions about the missing prices and fill in the menus.

How much is a hamburger?

A dollar forty-nine.

Hamburger	**$1.49**	French fries	small	
Cheeseburger			large	
Super Burger		Soft drink	small	.89
Chicken Sandwich	3.59		medium	1.09
Fish Sandwich	2.99		large	
Chicken Pieces		Coffee		.79
Salad bar	3.50	Apple pie		

Ordering Lunch

C. Read and practice.

Employee: Can I help you?

Customer: Sure. I'd like a chicken sandwich and a soda.

Employee: What size soda—small, medium, or large?

Customer: Medium.

Employee: Anything else?

Customer: Ummm. An order of large fries.

Employee: Is that it?

Customer: Yes.

Employee: For here or to go?

Customer: To go.

Employee: That's a chicken sandwich, a medium soda, and large fries. That's $6.37.

D. With a partner, write a new conversation. Order lunch from the menu above.

E. Group discussion. Sit in a group of three to four students. Talk about fast-food restaurants in your neighborhoods. Write the answers and report your information to the class.

Questions	Our Answers
1. Which fast-food restaurants are in your neighborhood?	
2. What is your favorite fast-food restaurant? Why?	
3. Which restaurant is cheap?	
4. Which restaurant is expensive?	
5. Which fast foods are good for you?	
6. Which fast-food restaurants are in your countries?	

F. Looking at fast-food facts. Guess the correct answer.

1. What is the most popular dessert in the U.S.?

   _____ cake _____ pie _____ ice cream _____ cookies _____ fruit

   What is *your* favorite dessert? _____

2. Put the ice cream flavors in the correct order of popularity from 1 to 4.

   _____ strawberry _____ chocolate _____ butter pecan _____ vanilla

   What is *your* favorite ice cream flavor? _____

3. What is the favorite ice cream topping?

   _____ pineapple   _____ strawberries

   _____ chocolate syrup   _____ whipped cream

   What is *your* favorite topping? _____

4. How many hamburgers do Americans eat in a week?

   a. one   **b.** two   **c.** three   **d.** four

5. Which country sells the most soda?

   a. Brazil   **b.** Mexico   **c.** the United States   **d.** China

   What's the most popular soda in *your* native country? _____

(Source: Beverage Marketing Corporation; International Ice Cream Association; T.G.I. Friday's/Harris Interactive/Yankelovich Partners)

Answers: 1. cookies 2. 1-vanilla; 2-chocolate; 3-butter pecan; 4-strawberry 3. chocolate syrup 4. a. one 5. c. the United States

A. Talk about the picture.

 B. Listen and label the people in the picture.

Jess	Harry	Mr. Lopez	Pete	Sherri
Kate	Mary	Patricia	Scott	Vera

C. Fill in the question words. Then, complete the answers.

1. __Who__ is working behind the counter?   Pete and Kate __are__.

2. _____ is Kate doing?   She _____ at the register.

3. _____ are Mary, Vera, and Patricia?   They _____ at Coffee to Go.

4. _____ are they doing?   They _____.

5. _____ is Mary drinking?   She _____ tea.

6. _____ is wiping tables?   Scott _____.

7. _____ is Harry talking to Scott?   Because Scott was late for work.

8. _____ is working?   Kate, Pete, and Scott _____.

D. Read and answer the questions.

Yes, she is. No, she isn't.	Yes, he is. No, he isn't.	Yes, she does. No, she doesn't.	Yes, he does. No, he doesn't.

1. Is Kate working overtime? _____
2. Is she tired? _____
3. Does Pete work at the donut shop? _____
4. Is Sherri taking a donut? _____
5. Does Jess come to the donut shop every day? _____
6. Does Jess always order the same thing? _____
7. Is Mary drinking coffee? _____
8. Is Scott mopping the floor? _____
9. Does Scott often come to work late? _____
10. Is Scott listening to his boss? _____

E. Write a story about the Coffee to Go donut shop.

Reading: Regional Favorites

A. Before You Read.

1. Does your native country or city have a famous food?
2. What city or state should you visit if you want to eat the best food?
3. Can you name a famous food from your city or state?

Pizza: New York City vs. Chicago

If you live in New York City, you probably eat New York style pizza. It has a thin crust, a thin layer of tomato sauce, and a layer of mozzarella cheese. Maybe you like to have sausage or pepperoni on your pizza, too. New York style pizza is not a heavy dish. It's so thin that you can fold it in half and eat it with one hand.

Chicago pizza is different. It is like a pie. It has a thick layer of cheese and other ingredients such as mushrooms, onions, and sausage. The fresh tomato sauce is on top, not on the bottom. Which is better? It depends. Are you from Chicago or from New York?

Chili: Cincinnati vs. Texas

Do you order your chili one-way, two-way, or maybe five-way? Then, you must be from Cincinnati, Ohio. In Cincinnati, chili is a combination of ground beef, tomato paste, onions, beans, and spices such as cinnamon and ginger. There are five different combinations. Here are two of them: "two-way" is chili on top of spaghetti; "three-way" is a two-way chili with cheese on top.

Do you put beans in chili? Not if you are from Texas. Typical Texas chili uses pieces of beef and spices for flavor. The spices and peppers are typical of dishes in Mexico.

B. Read and circle.

1. New York style pizza has a **thin / thick** crust.

2. Chicago style pizza has a **thin / thick** crust.

3. Which pizza is a heavy dish?   **a.** New York style   **b.** Chicago style

4. Which chili is served on spaghetti?   **a.** Cincinnati style   **b.** Texas style

5. Which chili has Mexican spices?   **a.** Cincinnati style   **b.** Texas style

6. Which chili is served five different ways? **a.** Cincinnati style   **b.** Texas style

 C. Make a list of five different countries and a popular food from each country.

Japan — sushi

A. Look at the pictures. Write a story. What is happening at the diner today? Is the restaurant busy? What are the employees doing? What are the customers doing?

_____

_____

_____

_____

_____

_____

_____

_____

_____

A. Contrast. Read and circle.

1. Are they preparing lunch?   (Now)   Every day
2. Who opens the store in the morning?   Now   Every day
3. Who's working at the counter?   Now   Every day
4. What do you do?   Now   Every day
5. What kind of sandwich are you eating? Now   Every day
6. Do you wear a uniform at work?   Now   Every day
7. What are you studying?   Now   Every day
8. Is she reading a book?   Now   Every day
9. Who's teaching your class?   Now   Every day

B. Read the story. Then, write the questions.

   Teresa is a counter clerk at Mr. Burger. This is her first day at the cash register, and she's very nervous. She's working slowly because she doesn't want to make a mistake. The restaurant is getting busy. Now there are six customers waiting in line. One man is getting impatient, and he's making Teresa more nervous. Patty is at the register, and Teresa is taking her order. Patty is ordering a fish sandwich meal and a drink. Patty's order is $4.50, and she's giving Teresa a $10 bill. Teresa is giving Patty $6.50 in change. Oops!

1. Who _____?   Teresa is.

2. How many customers _____?   Six.

3. Is _____?   No, she's working slowly.

4. Who _____?   One man is.

5. What _____?   A fish sandwich meal.

6. How much _____? $4.50.

7. How much _____? $10.00.

8. Is _____?   No, she isn't.

Looking at Numbers: Figuring out a Bill

A. Look at the menu on page 143. Figure out the total for each order.

1. Boris is ordering dinner. He wants a super burger, large French fries, and a large soda. How much is his order? _____

2. Tazuko is at Mr. Burger. She is ordering chicken pieces, the salad bar, and a small drink. How much is her order? _____

3. Joseph is ordering lunch for his children. He's ordering one order of chicken pieces, one cheeseburger, two orders of small fries, and two small drinks. How much is his order? _____

Grammar Summary

> **1. Present continuous**
> a. The present continuous describes an action that is happening now.
> b. Time expressions such as *now, right now, at this moment,* and *today* are often used with the present continuous.

> **2. *Yes/No* questions**

Am I work**ing**?	Yes, you are.	No, you aren't.	No, you're not.
Are you order**ing**?	Yes, I am.		No, I'm not.
Is he drink**ing** a soda?	Yes, he is.	No, he isn't.	No, he's not.
Is she eat**ing** a salad?	Yes, she is.	No, she isn't.	No, she's not.
Is it work**ing**?	Yes, it is.	No, it isn't.	No, it's not.
Are we pay**ing**?	Yes, we are.	No, we aren't.	No, we're not.
Are they cook**ing**?	Yes, they are.	No, they aren't.	No, they're not.

> **3. *Wh-* questions**

Where **am I** work**ing today**?	You're working in the kitchen.
Where **are you** work**ing**?	I'm working at the counter.
What **is he** order**ing**?	A muffin and coffee.
Why **is she** talk**ing** to the manager?	Because the employees are working slowly.
Where **are we** eat**ing** lunch?	At a fast-food restaurant.
What **are they** cook**ing**?	Eggs and bacon.

> **4. *Who* questions**   **Who** takes a singular verb form.

Who is working at the counter?	Teresa is.
Who is eating at the restaurant?	Mary, Patricia, and Vera are.

Food Shopping

Dictionary: Food

 A. Listen and repeat. Then, match the number and the item.

Produce

____ carrots	____ onions	____ bananas	____ pineapples	____ green beans
____ potatoes	____ broccoli	____ lettuce	____ peppers	____ tomatoes
____ apples	____ oranges	____ lemons	____ papayas	____ strawberries

Meat and Fish

____ chicken	____ pork chops	____ beef	____ hot dogs
____ ham	____ salmon	____ tuna	____ shrimp

Dairy

____ milk   ____ yogurt   ____ eggs   ____ butter/margarine   ____ cheese

Baked Goods

_____ bread   _____ donuts   _____ cookies   _____ cake   _____ pie

On the Shelves

_____ rice   _____ sugar   _____ peanut butter   _____ mayonnaise   _____ soup
_____ oil   _____ mustard   _____ salad dressing   _____ ketchup   _____ vinegar

Beverages

_____ coffee   _____ tea   _____ water   _____ soda   _____ juice

B. Answer.

1. What is your favorite food?

2. What foods do you like? What foods don't you like?

3. What food do you need to buy every week?

Active Grammar: Count and Non-count Nouns

Count Nouns

a donut

some donuts

an apple

some apples

Non-count Nouns

some water

some rice

some spaghetti

some milk

> Count nouns are items you can count. They can be singular or plural.
> Non-count nouns are items we cannot count. Do not use the plural *s*
> with non-count nouns.

A. Circle the items you can count.

(tomatoes)	an onion	donuts	oranges
cheese	yogurt	eggs	butter
salmon	carrots	a banana	bread
oil	hot dogs	cookies	sugar

B. Look at the food items. Write the names of two more items in each list.

Count Nouns		Non-count Nouns
Singular	**Plural**	
a donut	some donuts	some rice
a banana	some bananas	some lettuce

Making a Shopping List

A. Listen to this couple make a shopping list. Check (✓) the items they need.

		We need	We don't need
1.	milk	_____	✓
2.	hot dogs	_____	_____
3.	cheese	_____	_____
4.	lettuce	_____	_____
5.	a tomato	_____	_____
6.	a cucumber	_____	_____
7.	mayonnaise	_____	_____
8.	eggs	_____	_____
9.	an apple pie	_____	_____
10.	cookies	_____	_____

B. Talk about each item on the list above.

Count:	They need a tomato	They don't need a tomato.
	They need some apples.	They don't need any apples.
Non-count:	They need some rice.	They don't need any rice.

C. Complete.

1. Do we need any lettuce?

    Yes, we need _____ lettuce. And please buy _____ cucumber, too.

2. Do we need any mayonnaise?

    No, we don't need _____ mayonnaise. But please get _____ cheese.

3. Do we have hot dogs?

    We need _____ hot dogs. And we don't have _____ mustard.

4. How about dessert?

    Let's have _____ apple pie tonight. We don't need _____ cookies.

D. Read.

A: Let's make banana splits. We have a lot of ice cream.

B: Great idea. But we don't have any bananas.

A: We have some nuts. And we have some chocolate sauce.

B: But we don't have any whipped cream.

A: And we don't have any cherries for the top.

E. Complete with *some* or *any*.

A: Let's make an apple pie. We have _____ apples.

B: We don't have a pie crust. Let's buy a frozen one.

A: We don't have _____ sugar. We need _____ sugar and _____ butter.

B: And we don't have _____ vanilla ice cream for the top. Let's buy _____ .

F. Make a list of items you need for each recipe.

Pizza	Fruit salad
a pizza crust	

G. Write a dialogue. Talk about what you have and what you need to make one of the recipes in Exercise F.

Identifying Containers

A. Match the food below and the container. Add one more item to each list.

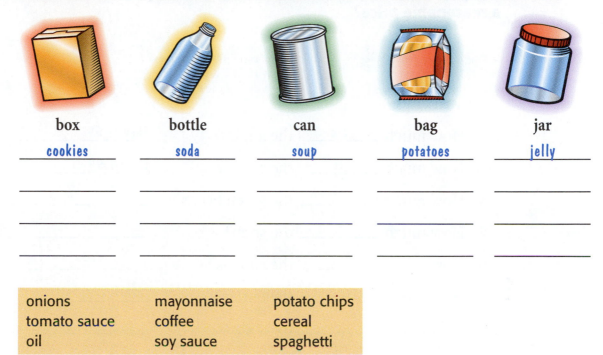

box	bottle	can	bag	jar
cookies	soda	soup	potatoes	jelly

onions	mayonnaise	potato chips
tomato sauce	coffee	cereal
oil	soy sauce	spaghetti

 B. Pronunciation: *of.* Listen and repeat.

1. a can of coffee
2. a jar of mustard
3. a bottle of ketchup
4. a box of cereal
5. a bag of cookies
6. a box of rice

Practice saying these food items with a partner.

1. a can of tuna fish
2. a jar of mayonnaise
3. a bottle of salad dressing
4. a box of crackers
5. a bag of onions
6. a box of macaroni

C. Complete. There are many kinds of containers. Can you complete these?

a gallon of _____   a six-pack of _____

a quart of _____   a package of _____

a container of _____   a slice of _____

A. Complete these questions and answers about prices. What is a reasonable price?

> How much is the lettuce?
> It's $1.29 a pound.

> How much are the onions?
> They're 59¢ a pound.

1. How much ___are___ the apples?   They're 69¢ _____ a pound.
2. How much ___is___ the coffee?   It's $4.99 _____ a pound.
3. How much _____ the green beans?   _____ a pound.
4. How much _____ the soup?   _____ a quart.
5. How much _____ the carrots?   _____ a pound.
6. How much _____ the butter?   _____ a pound.
7. How much _____ the soda?   _____ a bottle.
8. How much _____ the pears?   _____ a pound.
9. How much _____ the milk?   _____ a quart.
10. How much _____ the donuts?   _____ a dozen.

B. Ask and answer questions about these items, using *How much*. Decide on the prices together.

Working Together: Student to Student

A. Two supermarkets. Complete the chart about these two supermarkets.

STUDENT A: Ask Student B about prices at Shop and Save. Give prices for Food King.

STUDENT B: Turn to page 160.

How much are eggs at Shop and Save?

	Food King	Shop and Save
Eggs	79¢ a dozen	_____ a dozen
Butter	$2.19 a pound	_____ a pound
Chicken	$1.99 a pound	_____ a pound
Shrimp	$10.99 a pound	_____ a pound
Apples	69¢ a pound	_____ a pound
Cola	$1.69 a bottle	_____ a bottle
Bananas	49¢ a pound	_____ a pound

B. Two supermarkets. Complete the chart about these two supermarkets.

STUDENT B: Ask Student A about prices at Food King. Give prices for Shop and Save.

> How much are eggs at Food King?

	Food King	Shop and Save
Eggs	_____ a dozen	$1.19 a dozen
Butter	_____ a pound	$2.59 a pound
Chicken	_____ a pound	$2.39 a pound
Shrimp	_____ a pound	$7.99 a pound
Apples	_____ a pound	49¢ a pound
Cola	_____ a bottle	$1.39 a bottle
Bananas	_____ a pound	69¢ a pound

C. Use the information in your chart. Circle more or less.

1. Eggs are **more / less** expensive at Shop and Save.

2. Butter is **more / less** expensive at Shop and Save.

3. Chicken is **more / less** expensive at Shop and Save.

4. Shrimp is **more / less** expensive at Shop and Save.

5. Apples are **more / less** expensive at Shop and Save.

6. A bottle of cola _____.

7. Bananas _____.

D. Food brands. Complete this list with your favorite brands of these products. Compare your list with a small group. Explain why you prefer this brand.

coffee _____   tuna fish _____

yogurt _____   rice _____

mayonnaise _____   peanut butter _____

tomato sauce _____   soup _____

E. **What is she buying?** What is Mrs. Gibson buying? Write 10 sentences about her order.

1. <u>She's buying two boxes of rice.</u> _____

2. _____

3. _____

4. _____

5. _____

6. _____

7. _____

8. _____

9. _____

10. _____

The Big Picture: The Shopping List

A. Answer these questions about the picture.

1. Where are this man and woman?
2. What is their relationship?
3. What are they doing?

4. Who is going to do the shopping?
5. Who is making the list?
6. What is the woman looking at?

 B. Listen. This couple needs some food at the supermarket. Circle the items they need. Cross out the items they don't need.

apples	orange juice	toilet paper	spaghetti
bananas	apple juice	tissues	coffee
oranges	chicken	paper towels	peanut butter
pineapple	pork chops	cereal	vegetables
milk	beef	rice	ice cream

C. Complete with _a, some,_ or _any._

1. We need _____ fruit.

2. We have _____ oranges, but we don't have _____ apples.

3. We need _____ milk, but we don't need _____ orange juice.

4. Please get _____ can of coffee.

5. We have _____ beef, so we don't need _____.

6. We need _____ toilet paper, but we don't need _____ paper towels.

7. Please buy _____ jar of peanut butter and _____ box of spaghetti.

8. We don't need _____ cereal.

D. Coupons. Complete these sentences. Use your imagination for the new price.

1. Apples are 59¢ a pound. With the coupon, _they are 49¢ a pound._ _____

2. A can of tuna fish is $1.19. With the coupon, _____.

3. Milk is $1.19 a quart. With the coupon, _____.

4. Donuts are $3.29 a dozen. With the coupon, _____.

5. Ice cream is $3.79 a gallon. With the coupon, _____.

6. Pork chops are $4.29 a pound. With the coupon, _____.

E. Complete this conversation. You and your partner are roommates. What are you going to have for dinner? Make a list and complete the conversation.

A: What's for dinner tonight?

B: Let's make _____.

A: What do we need?

B: We need _____.

A: Do we need _____?

B: _____

A: _____

List

Reading: How to Make an Omelette

A. Vocabulary. You will need the following.

bowl   whisk   skillet   knife   grater   spatula

B. Label the ingredients.

pepper	ham
onion	eggs
salt	oil
pepper	cheese

C. Look at the recipe. Complete the information.

1.

Break the _____ into a bowl.

2.

Beat the _____.

3.

Chop the _____ and the _____.

4.

Slice the _____.

5.

Grate the _____.

6.
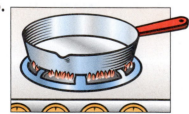

Heat the _____.

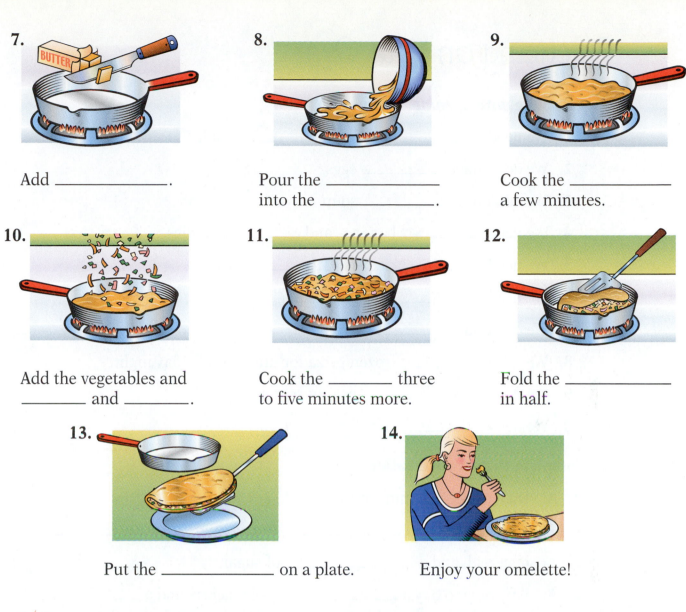

7. Add _____.

8. Pour the _____ into the _____.

9. Cook the _____ a few minutes.

10. Add the vegetables and _____ and _____.

11. Cook the _____ three to five minutes more.

12. Fold the _____ in half.

13. Put the _____ on a plate.

14. Enjoy your omelette!

Writing Our Recipes: Complete this recipe card with a favorite recipe.

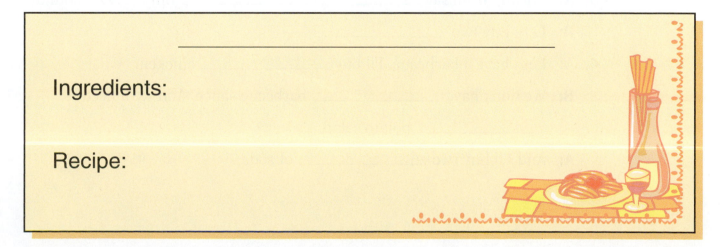

_____

Ingredients:

Recipe:

A. Complete with *a, some,* or *any.*

1. We need _____ cereal and _____ milk.

2. We don't have _____ eggs.

3. We don't have _____ soup.

4. We need _____ bananas and _____ apples.

5. We need _____ rice and _____ beans.

6. We need _____ six-pack of soda.

7. We don't have _____ oranges.

8. We need _____ frozen pizza for dinner on Friday night.

9. We don't have _____ peanut butter.

10. We need _____ cake for dessert.

B. Complete these conversations.

1. **A:** Do we need anything at the store?

   B: Yes, we need a _____ of mayonnaise, a _____ of cereal, and a _____ of sugar.

2. **A:** I'm going to buy a _____ of crackers and a _____ of jelly.

   B: Please get a _____ of peanut butter.

3. **A:** Shrimp is on sale. _____ _____ only $5.99 a pound.

   B: Let's buy two _____.

4. **A:** Let's have a barbecue. I'll buy _____ chicken.

   B: We don't have _____ barbecue sauce. And we'll need _____ potato salad.

   A: And I'll buy two _____ of soda.

Looking at Graphs: Favorite Vegetables

A. Americans list these five vegetables as their favorites. What vegetables do you like?

1. I like _____.

2. I don't like _____.

3. My favorite vegetable is _____.

4. Survey your class and find the five most popular vegetables.

Adults' Favorite Vegetables
1. Broccoli
2. Corn
3. Beans
4. Carrots
5. Potatoes

Grammar Summary

▶ 1. Count and non-count nouns

a. Count nouns are things we can count. Count nouns can be singular or plural.

    a donut   one donut   two donuts   three donuts   some donuts

b. Non-count nouns are things we can't count. We do not use the plural **s** with non-count nouns.

    rice   some rice   oil   some oil   milk   some milk

c. We can put food in containers and count the containers.

    a box of donuts   two boxes of donuts   a bag of rice   two bottles of oil

▶ 2. Count nouns

There is a donut in the box.

There are two donuts in the box.

There are some donuts in the box.

There aren't any donuts in the box.

Do we need any apples?

Apples are on sale. How much are they? They're 59¢ a pound.

▶ 3. Non-count nouns

There is some water in the cup.

There isn't any water in the cup.

Do we need any soda?

Soda is on sale. How much is it? It's 99¢ a bottle.

12 Last Weekend

Dictionary: Last Saturday

A. Listen and repeat.

studied	ordered	called
washed	visited	watched
worked out	cleaned	listened to

B. Maria was busy last Saturday. Complete these sentences about her day.

1.

In the morning, Maria ____cleaned____ her apartment.

2.

Then, she _____ her car.

3.

She _____ her favorite music as she worked.

4.

After lunch, she _____ for a test.

5.

Then, she _____ her sister.

6.

Later in the afternoon, she _____ at the gym.

7.

In the evening, she _____ her best friend.

8.

They _____ a pizza.

9.

They _____ a movie.

C. Past time expressions. Study these past time expressions. Then, complete the sentences.

last	ago	yesterday
last night	10 minutes ago	yesterday
last Sunday	an hour ago	yesterday morning
last weekend	three days ago	yesterday afternoon
last week	a week ago	yesterday evening
last month	a month ago	the day before yesterday
last year	a year ago	

1. Today is _____.

2. Yesterday was _____.

3. The day before yesterday was _____.

4. The year is _____.

5. Last year was _____.

6. Today's date is _____.

7. One week ago today was _____.

D. Last weekend. What did you do last weekend? Check the sentences that are true for you.

1. ☐ I cleaned my house.   6. ☐ I visited friends.

2. ☐ I washed my clothes.   7. ☐ I walked in the park.

3. ☐ I worked.   8. ☐ I washed my car.

4. ☐ I watched TV.   9. ☐ I studied.

5. ☐ I called my family.   10. ☐ I played _____.

E. Ask and answer questions about last weekend.

What did you do last weekend?

I cleaned my house.

Active Grammar: Past Tense of Regular Verbs

A Busy Morning

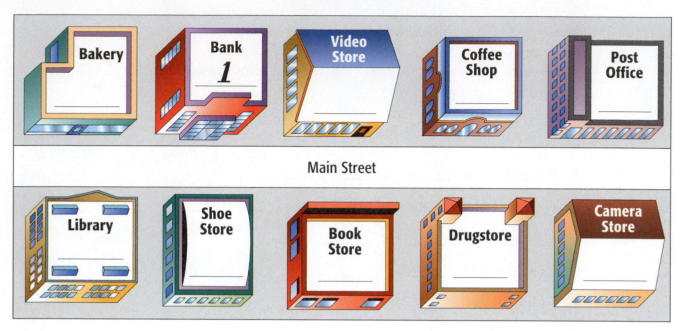

 A. Listen: Ali's morning. Ali went downtown on Saturday morning. Where did he go first, second, third, etc.? Number the locations from 1 to 8 on the map above.

B. Put Ali's morning in order.

_____ He picked up a prescription at the drugstore.

_____ Ali enjoyed a cup of coffee.

_____ He tried on some sneakers.

_____ He dropped off some film at the camera store.

__1__ Ali deposited his paycheck.

_____ He applied for a library card.

_____ He rented a movie.

_____ He mailed a letter to his brother.

Describe Ali's morning. Use _first, after that, then, next,_ and _finally._

C. Complete in the past tense.

rent
look at
walk
wait
stop
pick up
order
✓ walk
deposit
mail
talk

1. Ali _____*walked*_____ downtown.

2. He _____ his paycheck in the bank.

3. Ali _____ at the shoe store.

4. At the post office, he _____ a letter.

5. He _____ on line for ten minutes to buy stamps.

6. At the drugstore, he _____ to the pharmacist.

7. He _____ the pictures from his son's birthday party.

8. He _____ a movie.

9. He _____ juice, coffee, and a donut.

10. He _____ the newspaper from his country.

11. He _____ back home.

D. Pronunciation: Final -*ed*. Listen and repeat.

/d/		/t/		/əd/*	
play	played	walk	walked	need	needed
mail	mailed	stop	stopped	wait	waited
try	tried	look	looked	visit	visited

*When a verb ends in *t* or *d*, add a syllable to the verb.

Underline the verb in each sentence. Then, listen to the sentences on the tape. Write the number of syllables in the verb.

1. __1__ Ali <u>walked</u> to the bank.

2. _____ He wanted a pair of sneakers.

3. _____ Ali stopped at the shoe store.

4. _____ The manager helped him.

5. _____ Ali needed some stamps.

6. _____ Ali mailed a letter.

7. _____ He rented a movie.

8. _____ He picked up some film.

9. _____ Ali talked to a friend at the library.

10. _____ He looked at the newspaper.

Read the sentences with a partner.

E. Answer these questions about last weekend. Practice your pronunciation.

1. Did you study? Where did you study?

2. How long did you study?

3. Did you take a walk? Where did you walk?

4. Who did you visit?

5. Did you watch TV? What TV program did you watch?

6. What kind of music did you listen to?

7. Who did you call?

8. Did you work? Which days did you work?

9. Did you use a computer? What did you do? Did you play a game? Did you e-mail anyone?

10. Did you help anyone? What did you do?

11. Did you clean your house? What did you do?

12. What did you cook for dinner? Did you order any take-out food?

> Did you study?
> Yes, I did.
> No, I didn't.

F. Spelling: Past Tense

1. Most verbs: Add **-ed.**

open	open**ed**
mail	mail**ed**
walk	walk**ed**

2. Verbs that end with **e**: Add **-d.**

like	like**d**
close	close**d**
use	use**d**

3. Verbs that end in consonant + **y**: Change the **y** to **i**, add **-ed.**

study	stud**ied**
cry	cr**ied**
apply	appl**ied**

4. Verbs that end with a consonant, vowel, consonant: Double the final consonant.

stop	stop**ped**
shop	shop**ped**

   *Do not double final **w, x,** or **y.**
   fix   fix**ed**   play   play**ed**

Write the past tense.

clean _____   study _____

prepare _____   arrive _____

rent _____   stop _____

apply _____   visit _____

live _____   try _____

watch _____   want _____

Active Grammar: Past Tense of Irregular Verbs

Study these verbs! What is a good way to memorize them?

A. Listen and repeat.

be	was, were	fly	flew	say	said
begin	began	forget	forgot	see	saw
break	broke	get	got	send	sent
buy	bought	go	went	sit	sat
come	came	have	had	sleep	slept
do	did	know	knew	speak	spoke
drink	drank	leave	left	spend	spent
drive	drove	lose	lost	take	took
eat	ate	make	made	tell	told
fall	fell	pay	paid	think	thought
feel	felt	put	put	wear	wore
find	found	read	read	write	wrote

B. Answer.

1. What time did you get up today?
2. How did you feel when you got up?
3. What did you eat for breakfast?
4. What did you drink for breakfast?
5. What time did you leave your house?
6. How did you get to school? Did you take the bus?
7. What did you bring to school?
8. What did you forget?
9. What time did this class begin?
10. Who did you speak to before class?
11. How much did you pay for your pen?
12. What did you read yesterday?
13. Where did you go last night?
14. How many hours did you sleep last night?
15. What did you wear to school yesterday?

C. Talk about each picture. Use the past tense.

1.
2.
3.
4.
5.
6.

D. Negatives.

Sick in bed

   Bill didn't feel well on Thursday, but he went to work. By 12:00, he knew he was sick. He felt tired and hot. He had a bad headache. He spoke to his boss and asked to go home. When he got home, he took his temperature. It was 102°. Bill was in bed for the next three days.

Use the phrases below. What did Bill do this weekend? What didn't he do?

> **Past Tense: Negatives**
> Use **didn't** and the simple form of the verb.
>   He **didn't go** to work.
>   He **didn't visit** his friends.
>   He **didn't wash** the car.

work out at the gym   get a haircut

do his laundry

go to school   *watch TV*   take aspirin   drink juice

go to work   *do his homework*   cook

call the doctor   drink tea   take a walk   *sleep*

☀ How was your weekend?

A. Read and complete these complaints about air travel.

sick	broken	cold	late	uncomfortable
crowded	hot	terrible	dirty	

1. The plane was
_____.

2. The plane was
_____.

3. The seats were
_____.

4. The cabin was too
_____.

5. The woman in the next
seat was _____.

6. The food was
_____.

7. The weather was
_____.

8. My headset for the
movie was _____.

9. The bathrooms were
_____.

 B. Practice this conversation using different complaints from above.

A: Where were you on Friday? You weren't at work.

B: I took a day off. My son was in a soccer championship in Florida.

A: In Florida! Did you fly?

B: Yes. And the flight was terrible.

A: How come?

B: Well, _____.

C. Complete the conversation.

A: How was the game?

B: _____.

A: How were your seats?

B: _____. _____.

A: How was your son?

B: _____. He scored a goal. His team won!

D. Complain about each situation. Use *was* or *were*.

1. How was the restaurant?

   The food _____ too spicy.

   The service _____ too slow.

   The waiters _____ unfriendly.

2. How was the motel?

   The room _____ dirty and noisy.

   The beds _____ uncomfortable.

3. How was the weather?

   It _____ cloudy. It _____ cold and windy.

E. Complain about each of these situations or people. Use your imagination!

1. How was the traffic on your way to school today?

2. How was your last job? How was your last boss?

3. How was your last boyfriend / girlfriend?

4. How was your last test?

5. How was your weekend? Why?

A. **Irregular past quiz.** Give your book to your partner. Your partner will look at page 173 in your book and say the simple form of the verb. You will say the past form. With a light pencil, your partner will circle the verbs you need to study.

B. **My weekend.** Check the places you went last weekend. Then, tell your partner about each place and what you did there.

☐ the bank	☐ work	☐ a restaurant
☐ the post office	☐ the mall	☐ the supermarket
☐ the library	☐ the gym	☐ a friend's house
☐ the park	☐ the drugstore	☐ _____
☐ the travel agency	☐ school	☐ _____
☐ the laundromat	☐ the barber shop	☐ _____
☐ church	☐ the beauty parlor	

Where did you go last weekend?

I went to the park.

What did you do there?

I played soccer.

Write five sentences about your partner's weekend.

Example: Carlos went to the park and played soccer. _____

1. _____

2. _____

3. _____

4. _____

5. _____

A. Answer.

1. Did you ever get lost?

2. Where were you going?

3. Who gave you directions?

 B. Listen to the story about Paula. Then, answer the questions.

1. What time was the party?

2. What did Paula's friend give her?

3. What exit did she take?

4. Where did she leave her cell phone?

5. Who finally gave her directions?

6. What exit did she really want?

7. Did she have a good time at the party?

C. Match.

1. Paula tried to follow the directions,   a. but they couldn't give her the directions.
2. Paula spoke to several people,
3. Paula wanted to call,   b. but she really wanted Exit 15.
4. She tried to find a pay phone,   c. but she started to relax and enjoy the party.
5. Paula took Exit 14,
6. Paula wanted to arrive on time,   d. but she got lost.
7. At first she was upset,   e. but she arrived two hours late.
                                             f. but she didn't see one.
                                             g. but she left her cell phone at home.

D. Complete in the past tense. Some of the sentences are negative.

1. A friend from work _____invited_____ Paula to a birthday party.
2. Her friend _____didn't give_____ her the correct directions.
3. Paula _____ her house early.
4. She _____ the directions carefully.
5. She _____ to have problems.
6. She _____ several people for directions.
7. She _____ the wrong exit.
8. Paula _____ her cell phone with her.
9. She _____ a pay telephone.
10. A police officer _____ her the right directions.

see
begin
ask
take
✓ give
have
leave
✓ invite
follow
give

E. Paula and her friend are talking. Put their conversation in order. Practice with another student.

_____ I'm really sorry! How did you find the street?

_____ I got lost.

___1___ Paula, you're here! What happened?

_____ I did. But you wrote Exit 14. You meant Exit 15.

_____ I finally found a police officer and asked him.

_____ Did you follow the directions?

Reading: The Iowa State Fair

A. Before You Read. Look at the map. Circle these locations at the Iowa State Fair.

Heritage Village	Ferris Wheel	Sky Glider	Sheep Barn
Race Track	Agriculture Building	Poultry Building	Grandfather's Farm
Midway	Horse Barn	Machinery Grounds	Riley Stage

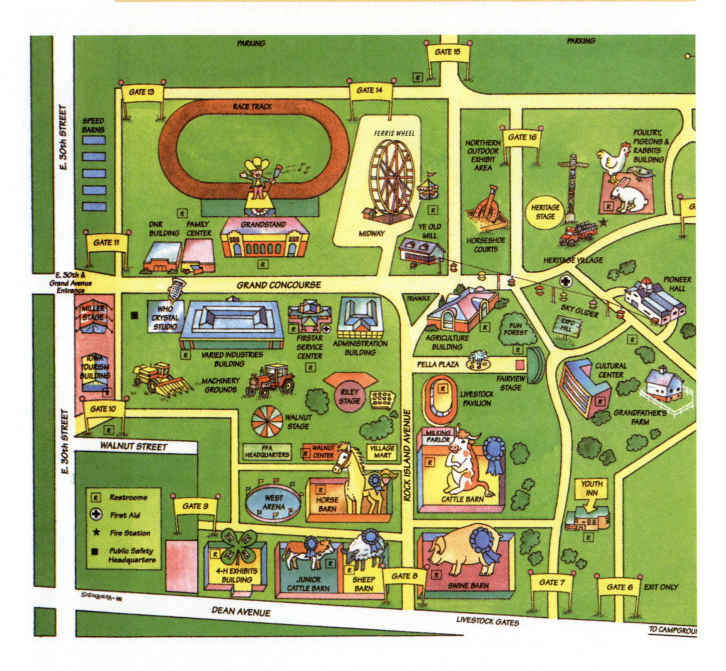

You can visit the Iowa State Fair on the Internet at www.iowastatefair.org.

B. These are some activities at a state fair. Can you explain each?

shows	car races	rides	fair
exhibits	competitions	fireworks	contests

The Iowa State Fair

"I couldn't believe my eyes!", said Pablo Ospina. "I expected a small fair with rides and animals. I loved it! I went to the fair with a friend on Friday night. Then, I drove back with my family on Saturday and again on Sunday."

Pablo is talking about the Iowa State Fair, one of the largest state fairs in the United States. This year the Fair was 10 days long and almost one million visitors attended. The first Iowa State Fair was in 1854, on a small farm. Farmers came together and talked about farming, animals, and new ideas. Today the Fair is the size of a small town. It's not only for farmers. City and country people enjoy the many entertainment shows, the car and horse races, many rides, hundreds of exhibits and competitions, and the fireworks at night.

Pablo enjoyed the contests. He watched the Pie Eating Contest. The winner ate two pies in ten minutes. He laughed at the Mother and Daughter Look-a-Like Contest. He listened to the Guitar-Playing Contest.

Pablo's wife, Nancy, is a gardener. In the Agriculture Building, she looked at the largest tomato and the biggest peppers. She saw beautiful vegetables, apples, cheese, popcorn, ham, and other farm products. She watched the competition for the most beautiful roses.

Pablo's two boys wanted to see Heritage Village. Grandfather's Farm showed farm life in early times. They went into the old-fashioned general store, the country schoolhouse and the barber shop. The boys also liked all the animals, so they stopped at the Horse Barn and the Sheep Barn. They watched how to milk a cow and how to make butter. Of course, the boys went on many rides at the Midway, such as the Ferris Wheel and the Sky Glider.

Everyone was hungry and thirsty all day. They stopped every hour and tried different food. The most popular kind of food at the fair was food-on-a-stick. They tried chicken-on-a-stick, pork chop-on-a-stick, and fried candy-bar-on-a-stick. Later in the afternoon, the family walked to the race track and watched car races. They stayed for the fireworks in the evening. Everyone had a great time. Pablo is already planning to return for next year's fair.

C. <u>Underline</u> each place this family visited at the state fair.

Writing Our Stories:
A Special Weekend

Write about a special weekend that you enjoyed with friends or family. Where did you go? What did you do? Give many examples.

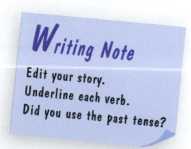

Writing Note

Edit your story.
Underline each verb.
Did you use the past tense?

A. Past tense. Complete this story with the past tense of the verbs.

My wife and I go out almost every Saturday. Sometimes we go to a restaurant, a movie, or to a party. We think it's good to relax after a hard week's work.

Last Saturday, we _____**did**_____ (do) our chores in the morning. We _____ (clean) our house and _____ (go) food shopping. After that, we _____ (visit) my wife's parents. We _____ (get) home by 5:00, so we _____ (decide) to go out for dinner. We _____ (eat) at Faroles Restaurant and we _____ (have) Spanish food.

It _____ (be) a little uncomfortable for us in the restaurant because we _____ (have) our daughter with us. Lizzie is only 20 months old and is sometimes very noisy. She _____ (say) "Hi!" to everyone. Thankfully, she _____ (sit) quietly under our table most of the time!

After we _____ (finish) dinner, we _____ (drive) to the park. We _____ (put) Lizzie in her stroller and we _____ (walk) around the lake. It _____ (be) so beautiful and quiet. My daughter _____ (fall) asleep in her stroller.

B. Negatives. Complete these sentences about the story in Exercise A. Write the verbs in the negative.

They _____**didn't go**_____ out on Friday night; they went out on Saturday night.

They _____ his wife's sister; they visited his wife's parents.

They _____ in an Indian restaurant; they ate at a Spanish restaurant.

Their daughter _____ in a chair; she sat under the table.

They _____ to a movie; they went to the park.

Their daughter _____ asleep in the car; she fell asleep in her stroller.

They _____ home late; they got home early.

Looking at Graphs: State Fair Attendance

A. Look at the chart and talk about fair attendance in 2000.

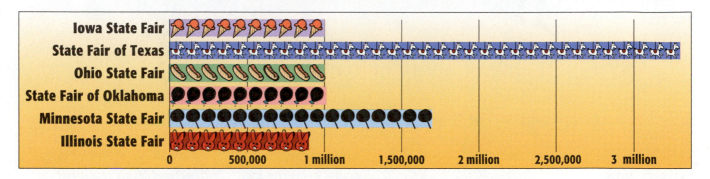

The _____ was very popular.

The _____ had _____ visitors in 2000.

The _____ had the most visitors in 2000.

Grammar Summary

▶ **1. Past tense**

Use the simple past tense to talk about things you did in the past.

Regular past tense verbs end with **-ed:**   walk**ed**   play**ed**   visit**ed**

The chart of irregular past verbs is on page 173.

▶ **2. Statements**

I We You They He She It	cook**ed** enjoy**ed** prepar**ed** **ate** **made**	dinner.

▶ **3. Negatives**

I We You They He She It	**did not** **didn't**	cook enjoy prepare eat make	dinner.

13 Growing Up

Dictionary: Important Events

 A. Listen and repeat the regular past tense verbs and verb phrases.

celebrate a birthday	**celebrated** a birthday	move to another state	**moved** to another state
change jobs	**changed** jobs	retire from my job	**retired** from my job
die	**died**	return to my country	**returned** to my country
graduate from high school	**graduated** from high school	study English	**studied** English

B. Write a past tense verb phrase in Exercise A under the correct picture.

1. _____
_____

2. _____

3. _____

4. _____

5. _____

6. _____

C. Irregular verbs. Listen and repeat the irregular verbs.

began	fell	got	had	met
came	found	✓grew up	made	went

D. Look at the pictures. Then, write the correct verbs.

1. Laura _____grew up_____ in Lima, Peru.

2. She _____ to the U.S. in August 1999.

3. She _____ a job at the Tropicana Restaurant.

4. She _____ English classes at the local college.

5. Laura _____ her future husband, Luca, in her class.

6. After one month, they _____ in love.

7. Laura _____ engaged to Luca on February 14, 2000.

8. Luca _____ the local soccer team.

9. Laura and Luca _____ married December 31, 2000.

10. Laura and Luca _____ on a honeymoon to Peru.

Yes/No Questions – Did	
Did you	take a vacation?
	get married?
	get your license?

A. Read and ⟨circle.⟩

1. Did you take a vacation last year? Yes, I did. No, I didn't.

2. Did you move to a new apartment last month? Yes, I did. No, I didn't.

3. Did you get married last year? Yes, I did. No, I didn't.

4. Did you begin English classes last week? Yes, I did. No, I didn't.

5. Did you get married two years ago? Yes, I did. No, I didn't.

6. Did you have a baby five years ago? Yes, I did. No, I didn't.

7. Did you go back to your country last winter? Yes, I did. No, I didn't.

8. Did you get a driver's license last year? Yes, I did. No, I didn't.

B. Pair practice. Ask and answer the questions with a partner.

Past Tense Expressions

last month	one year ago
last week	two years ago
last year	in 2000

Did you celebrate a birthday last month?

Yes, I did.

No, I didn't. My birthday is in September.

celebrate something important

move to a new place

change jobs

go to your country

take a vacation

come to the U.S. in 2000

C. Look at the pictures. Talk about these important events in Alex's life.

1995

1996

1998

2000

2002

 D. Listen and complete the questions. Then, write the answers.

1. Did Alex ___come to the U.S.___ in ___1985___?   ___No, he didn't___

2. Did Alex _____ to New York in _____?   _____

3. Did Alex _____ in _____?   _____

4. Did Alex _____ with Lena in _____?   _____

5. Did they _____ in _____?   _____

☀ Asking *Who* Questions

 A. Listen and answer.

Answers
Paul did.
Marta did.

Paul

Marta

1. Who grew up in El Salvador?

2. Who went to nursing school?

3. Who got a job at a bank?

4. Who worked at a hospital?

5. Who worked in New York City?

6. Who changed jobs?

B. Look at the pictures. Ask and answer the questions with a partner.

Who grew up in the U.S.?
Janet Jackson did.

Who played tennis?
Steffi Graf did.

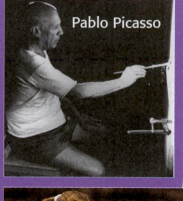
Pablo Picasso

Janet Jackson

1. Who performed with her brothers?

2. Who lived in Spain?

3. Who was born in Hong Kong?

4. Who sold many CDs?

5. Who won many tennis matches?

6. Who painted famous art works?

7. Who studied Kung Fu?

8. Who grew up in Germany?

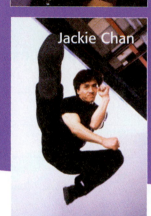
Jackie Chan

Steffi Graf

☀ Asking *Wh-* Questions

C. Read.

A: Where were you born?
B: **I was born in Russia.**
A: When did you come to this country?
B: **I came here in 1998.**
A: Who came with you?
B: **My husband and my children did.**
A: Did you understand English?
B: **No, I didn't.**
A: How did you learn English?
B: **I went to an English class, and I watched TV programs in English.**

 D. Practice the dialogue above. Talk about your life.

 188   UNIT 13

E. Complete the questions. Ask and answer the questions with a partner.

did	were	born	come
live	find	grow up	learn

1. Where _____were_____ you _____born_____?

2. Where _____did_____ you _____grow up_____?

3. When _____ you _____ to this country?

4. Why _____ you _____ to this country?

5. How _____ you _____ to this country?

6. How _____ you _____ English?

7. When _____ you _____ a job?

8. Where _____ you _____ after you came here?

F. My teacher. Complete these past tense questions. Ask your teacher about his/her life.

1. Where _____were_____ you born?

2. Where _____did_____ you _____?

3. What _____ you _____?

4. What university _____ you _____?

5. When _____ you _____?

6. How _____ you _____?

7. Why _____ you _____?

Write three more questions for your teacher.

8. _____?

9. _____?

10. _____?

☀ Talking About a Party

A. Read and put the sentences in order from 1–10.

_____ **a.** Then, I invited my friends.

_____ **b.** I went to a party store.

_____ **c.** I went to the supermarket.

_____ **d.** Next, I prepared the food.

___1___ **e.** First, I made a guest list.

_____ **f.** I bought decorations.

_____ **g.** After that, I made a shopping list.

_____ **h.** I bought food and drinks.

_____ **i.** Finally, my friends arrived, and we had a great time.

_____ **j.** Then, I decorated my apartment.

> First,
>
> Then,
> Next,
> After that,
>
> Finally,

B. Look at the pictures and tell the story. Use _first, then, after that, next,_ and _finally._

received / visa

told / family

told / parents

bought

packed

went

flew

met

C. In your notebook, write a story about the pictures in Exercise B.

Writing Note

Put a comma after _First,_ and _Next,_ at the beginning of a sentence.

D. Pronunciation: *Did you* and *Did he*. Listen and repeat.

| Did you = Did_you | Did he = Did_he |

1. Did you change jobs?
2. Did you get married?
3. Did you find a job?
4. When did you find a job?
5. What did you do yesterday?

6. Did he study English?
7. Did he get divorced?
8. Did he go back to his country?
9. How did he get there?
10. Why did he go back?

 Practice asking these questions with a partner.

Working Together: Student to Student

A. STUDENT A: Listen to Student B. Write questions 1 to 3. Then, read questions 4 to 6.

STUDENT B: Turn to page 192. Read questions 1 to 3.

1. _____ On July 8th.
2. _____ At a church.
3. _____ At 3:00.

4. Where did they have the reception?
5. How many people did they invite?
6. How much did the wedding cost?

B. STUDENT B: Read questions 1 to 3. Then, listen to Student A. You will write questions 4 to 6.

1. When did they get married?

2. Where did they get married?

3. What time did the ceremony begin?

4. _____ At a restaurant.

5. _____ 175 people.

6. _____ $6,000.

C. A timeline. Think of five important dates and events in your life. Then, write the dates in the boxes in chronological order. Write one sentence next to each date.

	_____
	_____
	_____
	_____
	_____

Tell your partner about your life.

D. Find someone who . . . Walk around the classroom and ask questions about growing up.

Did you go to high school in the United States?
No, I didn't. (Ask another person.)

Did you go to high school in the United States?
Yes, I did. (Write the name.)

Find someone who . . .	Classmate
1. went to high school in this country.	_____
2. had a pet.	_____
3. spent time with his or her grandparents.	_____
4. wore a uniform to school.	_____
5. won a competition.	_____
6. went to a lot of parties.	_____
7. attended a university in his / her native country.	_____
8. lived in another state.	_____

E. Memories. Bring in a photograph of an important day in your life. Tell a group of classmates about that day. What happened? Your classmates will ask you questions.

How did you break your leg?
Did you stay in the hospital?
How long did you wear a cast?
Did you stay home from school?
Who helped you?

The Big Picture: Growing Up

A. Listen and look at the pictures.

B. Listen again. Talk about Oscar's life.

C. Listen and circle.

1. a. Texas   b. El Salvador   c. Mexico

2. a. He fell out of bed.   b. He fell off a bicycle.   c. He fell in love.

3. a. In second grade   b. In seventh grade   c. In sixth grade

4. a. When he was 10   b. When he was 12   c. When he was 2

5. a. Detroit   b. Denver   c. Dallas

6. a. A little   b. A lot   c. None

7. a. When he was 15   b. When he was 16   c. When he was 17

8. a. His mother did.   b. The manager did.   c. His father did.

D. Ask and answer *Yes/No* questions about Oscar and about your life.

1. Did Oscar break his arm?

2. Did Oscar have the measles?

3. Did Oscar move to the United States with his family?

4. Did Oscar play a sport in high school?

5. Did Oscar fall in love in high school?

6. Did you break your arm or leg?

7. Did you work when you were in high school?

8. Did you have chicken pox?

9. Did you play a sport in high school?

10. Did you fall in love in high school?

E. Complete these questions. Then, answer the questions.

Who	What	When	Where	Why	How	Did

1. _____How_____ many times a week did he play soccer?

2. _____ taught Oscar to drive?

3. _____ he get his license when he was 16?

4. _____ did he go to school?

5. _____ did he win when he was a child?

6. _____ did he get his first job?

7. _____ did he get a job?

8. _____ he like high school at first?

9. _____ did he do after high school?

10. _____ old is Oscar?

Reading: Jackie Chan

A. Before You Read

1. Who is Jackie Chan?
   What country is he from?

2. Can you name the title of one
   of Jackie Chan's movies?

(1) <u>Jackie Chan was born on April 7, 1954, in Hong Kong.</u> His parents left mainland China for Hong Kong a short time before he was born. His parents named him "Chan Kong-sang", which means "born in Hong Kong." They wanted to celebrate a safe trip to Hong Kong.

At first, Jackie's family lived in the French Embassy. His father was a cook, and his mother was a housekeeper. When Jackie was seven years old, his family moved to Australia. His father got a job as head chef in the American Embassy. Later, back in Hong Kong, Jackie's father sent Jackie to the China Drama Academy. Jackie studied and worked 19 hours a day. The students practiced Kung Fu and learned how to do many stunts, such as flips and somersaults.

When Jackie was 17, he began to perform dangerous stunts for movies. In the early 1980s, Jackie went to Hollywood, but he wasn't very successful. He continued to make movies in Hong Kong and had great success. Finally, in 1995, Jackie Chan became famous in the United States with his movie, "Rumble in the Bronx." Today, Jackie Chan has both Chinese and American fans, and his movies make millions of dollars.

B. Underline the answers to these questions.

1. Where was Jackie Chan born?

2. What was his father's occupation?

3. Where did Jackie Chan study Kung Fu?

4. Was his first trip to Hollywood successful?

5. What was the name of Jackie Chan's first successful Hollywood movie?

Writing Our Stories: Coming to the United States

A. Read.

I came to the United States from Cuba two years ago. I came here with my two sons. My father was here in Florida, so my sons and I found an apartment in Florida, too.

In Cuba, I studied to be a pharmacist. I worked in a hospital. My family and my friends helped me a lot. I was never alone.

At first, I had a problem with English. I couldn't understand people. I couldn't find a good job and use my education. I had to go to school to learn how to communicate. Also, I wanted to bring my mother here, but I had to find a good job and a place to live.

Now, many things are different. I have a good job in a pharmaceutical company. I study at a college and I can communicate in English. My mother is here now, and my sons speak English very well. It's not easy, but I like my life very much.

Liliana

B. Complete.

1. I came to this country on _____.
   _{date}

2. I arrived **on foot** / **by air** / **by boat.**

3. I came **alone** / **with** _____.

4. I **knew** / **didn't know** English.

C. In your notebook, write about your move to this country.

A. Read.

When I came to this country three years ago, I didn't know how to drive. Bus service wasn't good, so I needed to drive to get to my job. My brother taught me how to drive. Every weekend, he took me to the high school parking lot. I practiced going straight, backing up, turning, stopping, and parking. After six weeks, I took the driving test at the Department of Motor Vehicles. I made a lot of mistakes. I forgot to signal when I turned, I didn't stop at a stop sign, and I didn't park correctly. I failed the test. After that, I practiced in my neighborhood and downtown. Four weeks later, I passed the test.

B. Put the words in the questions in the correct order. Then, answer the questions.

1. to this country / did / come / when / Julia

   _____?

2. good / the bus service / was

   _____?

3. Julia / did / need / a driver's license / why

   _____?

4. taught / Julia / who / how to drive

   _____?

5. where / Julia / practice / did

   _____?

6. pass / the first time / the test / Julia / did

   _____?

Looking at Graphs: A Survey

A. Complete this graph about the students in your class.

Write six countries represented in your class.	Write the number of students.	Complete the graph. Color in one block for each number.
_____	_____	
_____	_____	
_____	_____	
_____	_____	
_____	_____	
_____	_____	

1 2 3 4 5 6 7 8 9 10

Grammar Summary

▶ **1. *Yes/No questions***

Did you **study** English?   Yes, I **did.**

Did he **come** to the country alone?   No, he **didn't.**

▶ **2. *Who questions***

Who **came** here with you?   My parents **did.**

Who **changed** jobs?   I **did.**

▶ **3. *Wh- questions***

What did you do yesterday?

Where did you live?

How did she find a job?

When did they get married?

Why did he come to this country?

14 Weekend Plans

Dictionary: Weekend Activities

A. Listen and repeat.

Actions at Home

go out	have a party	eat out	stay home	watch TV	work
get up early	do homework	sleep late	read a book	study	visit friends

B. Write the verb or verb phrase under the correct picture.

1. _____

2. _____

3. _____

4. _____

5. _____

6. _____

7. _____

8. _____

9. _____

10. _____

11. _____

12. _____

C. Listen and repeat.

Celebrations

an anniversary

a birthday

a graduation

a wedding

Sports and Entertainment

play baseball

play cards

play soccer

play volleyball

Actions with *Go*

go dancing

go running

go shopping

go swimming

Chores at Home

iron my clothes

do the laundry

do the shopping

vacuum the living room

Active Grammar: Future Tense

A. Listen and complete.

1. <u>He's going to do</u> _____ the laundry.

2. _____ the dishes.

3. _____ the carpet.

4. _____ a birthday.

5. _____ volleyball.

6. _____ homework.

B. Read the chart. Make sentences about your plans.

> I am going to read a book tonight.
> They are going to get up early on Saturday.
> My family and I are going to watch TV tonight.
> She is going to celebrate her birthday next week.

Future: be + going to + verb

I	am			
You			read a book	tomorrow.
We			go out with friends	tonight.
They	are		get up early	this weekend.
My family and I		going to	go dancing	on Saturday.
			go to bed late	on Sunday
			go to work	next week.
He			watch TV	next month.
She	is		celebrate a birthday	next year.
It			visit friends	in a few minutes.
				in an hour.

C. Write five of your sentences from Exercise B.

1. _____

2. _____

3. _____

4. _____

5. _____

D. Look at the pictures. With a partner, ask and answer questions about the pictures.

What is he going to do?

He's going to see the dentist.

What's she going to do?
What's he going to do?
What are they going to do?

call the police	sing "Happy Birthday!"
get a shot	take an exam
go to bed	take a trip
see the dentist	

1.

2.

3.

4.

5.

6.

7.

Use your imagination with these pictures.

1.

2.

3.

E. Pronunciation: *going to* **versus** */gonna/.* Listen and repeat the slow form, *going to,* and the reduced form */gonna/.*

1. Tom**'s going to take** a test tomorrow.

2. Ellen**'s going to have** a baby in January.

3. Steven**'s going to study** for a test.

4. Venus **is going to play** a tennis match.

5. You**'re going to buy** a new car.

6. I**'m going to do** the laundry.

7. They **aren't going to get** married next year.

8. We**'re not going to take** a trip next month.

9. She**'s not going to cook** dinner tonight.

10. I**'m not going to eat** dessert this week.

> *Going to* is pronounced [gonna] in natural speech. Do not write **gonna**.

 Practice saying both forms with a partner.

 F. Listen and complete.

1. I _____ my car tomorrow.

2. The students _____ after class.

3. Some students _____ homework tonight.

4. Our teacher _____ next week.

5. The school _____ for the holidays.

6. They _____ late tomorrow morning.

7. The class _____ next month.

8. I _____ at 11 o'clock.

 Practice saying these sentences with a partner.

G. Listen to Mariana's plans. Circle the activities that she's going to do. Cross out the activities that she's *not* going to do.

H. Complete the sentences about Mariana's weekend. Some of the sentences are negative.

clean	do	✓ get up	sleep
cook	eat	go	study

1. Mariana _____ is going to get up _____ early.

2. She _____ her apartment.

3. She _____ her laundry.

4. She _____ in her apartment.

5. She _____ to the library.

6. Mariana _____ the supermarket.

7. Mariana _____ a special meal.

8. Mariana and her boyfriend _____
   at a restaurant.

9. They _____ at her apartment.

A. Find someone who . . . Ask your classmates questions about their plans. If the answer is "Yes," write the student's name on the blank. If the answer is "No," ask another student.

	Question	Classmate
1.	Are you going to take a vacation this year?	_____
2.	Are you going to celebrate a birthday this month?	_____
3.	Are you going to exercise tomorrow?	_____
4.	Are you going to clean your house this weekend?	_____
5.	Are you going to go dancing on Saturday night?	_____
6.	Are you going to get up early on Sunday morning?	_____
7.	Are you going to study this weekend?	_____
8.	Are you going to visit friends this weekend?	_____

B. Weekend plans. Check (✓) your plans for this weekend. Then, read your sentences to your partner. Check your partner's plans.

Weekend Plans	You		Your partner	
	Yes	No	Yes	No
1. I'm going to get up early this weekend.				
2. I'm going to stay home this weekend.				
3. I'm going to work this weekend.				
4. I'm going to play a sport this weekend.				
5. I'm going to do the shopping this weekend.				

C. Complete the sentences about you and your partner.

1. I _____ get up early.

2. My partner _____ get up early.

3. I _____ stay home this weekend.

4. My partner _____ stay home this weekend.

5. My partner and I _____.

D. What are their plans for the future? Talk about these famous people's plans.

He's going to make a movie.
She's going to give a concert.

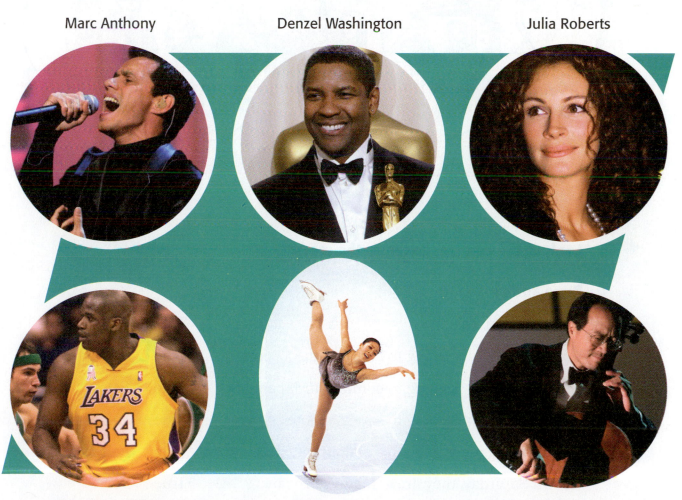

Marc Anthony

Denzel Washington

Julia Roberts

Shaquille O'Neal

Michelle Kwan

Yo Yo Ma

The Big Picture: A Visitor

A. **Look at the picture. Masa Ohtani is looking forward to his mother's visit. Talk about his plans.**

 B. **Look at the picture. Listen to the story.**

C. **Read and ⟨circle.⟩**

1.	Masa is tired.	True	⟨False⟩
2.	Mrs. Ohtani is going to arrive at the airport.	True	False
3.	Mrs. Ohtani is going to come from Japan.	True	False
4.	Mrs. Ohtani is going to stay at a hotel.	True	False
5.	They are going to go to a restaurant.	True	False
6.	On Saturday, they are going to sleep late.	True	False
7.	Mrs. Ohtani is going to get married next year.	True	False
8.	Mrs. Ohtani is going to meet Masa's girlfriend.	True	False

D. Read and put the plans in order from 1 to 6.

_____ a. Mrs. Ohtani is going to meet his girlfriend.

_____ b. Masa is going to meet his mother at the airport.

_____ c. They're going to have dinner with his sister.

_____ d. They're going to sleep late.

___1___ e. Masa's going to clean his apartment.

_____ f. Masa's going to take his mother around San Francisco.

E. Read each sentence. Correct the sentence. Say the sentence again.

1. Masa's father is going to come for a visit.

> Masa's **father** isn't going to come for a visit.
> Masa's **mother** is going to come for a visit.

2. His mother is going to stay for a month.

3. She's going to arrive at the Oakland airport.

4. She's going to stay in a hotel.

5. They're going to drive to his brother's house.

6. On Saturday, they're going to get up early.

7. They're going to visit the art museum.

8. Masa's going to get married next month.

F. What are you going to do? A friend from your country is going to visit you next week. What are you going to do? Complete the sentences.

1. I am going to pick him up at the airport._____

2. I _____

3. We _____

4. We _____

5. We _____

A. Before You Read.

1. Is your country going to host an Olympics some time in the future?

2. Did your country ever host the Olympics?

3. Do you know someone who is going to participate in the Olympics?

Every two years, the Winter or the Summer Olympic Games take place. It is a great honor for a country to have the Olympics. Many countries want to host the Olympics, so it is very competitive to get the Games.

The International Olympic Committee, or the I.O.C., chooses the city for the Olympics. When a city decides that it wants to host the Olympic Games, it makes a committee of local residents. Then, there are many questions that the I.O.C. asks the committee.

1. Is your city going to have good transportation to the Olympic events?

2. Is the city going to have enough hotels for the visitors?

3. Who's going to be responsible for security?

4. Is the weather going to be good for the events?

5. Is the public going to support the Olympics?

6. Which airport are the visitors going to use?

7. What facilities does the city have now? What facilities is the city going to build?

8. How is the city going to pay for this project?

For many cities, it is very expensive to have the Olympics. For example, if a city has an old stadium, it is probably going to build a big, new stadium. If a city doesn't have enough hotels, it is going to build more hotels.

B. You and your committee want to hold the Olympics in your city. How is your city going to prepare for the Games? With a group of students, prepare a proposal for the Summer or Winter Olympic Games. Each group is going to present its proposal to the "I.O.C." Choose another group of students to be the "I.O.C." They are going to select the winner.

Writing Our Stories: My Weekend Plans

A. Read.

This weekend, I'm going to have a surprise party for my wife. We're going to have a cake, ice cream, and some punch. On Saturday morning, she's going to go to work. She doesn't know anything about the party. I'm going to clean our apartment. Then, I'm going to wrap her present in a special box. It's a pair of airline tickets to our native country. Our children are going to decorate the apartment. They're going to give her presents, too. We're going to have a great party on Saturday night.

B. Write about your weekend plans.

This weekend, I am going to _____.

_____ On Saturday morning, I _____

_____

In the afternoon, _____

In the evening, _____

On Sunday morning, _____.

_____ On Sunday evening, I

_____

Writing Note

Use a comma after a time expression at the beginning of a sentence.

On Saturday evening, we're going to see a movie.

Practicing on Your Own

A. Contrast: future, present, and present continuous. Read and circle.
What time does the sentence describe?

1. The children are watching TV.	(Now)	Future	Every day
2. He works at an express delivery company.	Now	Future	Every day
3. They're going to buy a new car this year.	Now	Future	Every day
4. She is vacuuming her apartment.	Now	Future	Every day
5. Belinda is going to make a salad for dinner.	Now	Future	Every day
6. I eat cereal and fruit for breakfast.	Now	Future	Every day
7. We're preparing our house for a party.	Now	Future	Every day
8. The students are going to take a test.	Now	Future	Every day

B. Contrast: future, present, and present continuous. Read and complete the sentences about an English class. Pay attention to the time expressions.

arrive	begin	do	end	go
listen	play	take	visit	write

1. Our class _____ begins _____ at 9:00 every morning.

2. One student _____ late for class every day.

3. The students _____ a test tomorrow.

4. Right now, the teacher _____ a tape recorder.

5. The students _____ to a tape about the news in a few minutes.

6. The students _____ to the computer lab once a week.

7. The students _____ a lot of homework tonight.

8. At the moment, the teacher _____ on the chalkboard.

9. Next month, the students _____ a museum.

10. Our class always _____ at 12:00.

Looking at Graphs: Favorite Weekend Activities

A. Read the graph. What do people like to do on weekends? Complete the sentences with the correct percentages.

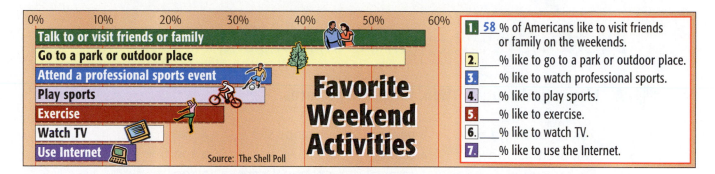

Source: The Shell Poll

Favorite Weekend Activities

1. **58** % of Americans like to visit friends or family on the weekends.
2. ____ % like to go to a park or outdoor place.
3. ____ % like to watch professional sports.
4. ____ % like to play sports.
5. ____ % like to exercise.
6. ____ % like to watch TV.
7. ____ % like to use the Internet.

B. What is your favorite weekend activity?

Grammar Summary

▶ **1. Future tense statements**

Use **be + going to** to talk about actions in the future.

I **am going to take** a vacation next month.

She **is going to have** a baby in January.

We **are going to buy** a new car tomorrow.

They **are not going to look** for a new apartment this year.

You **are not going to work** overtime on Saturday.

▶ **2. Future time expressions**

Put the time expressions at the beginning or at the end of a sentence.

Tomorrow morning, I'm going to get up early.

She's going to visit her brother **next week.**

tonight	tomorrow	tomorrow night	the day after tomorrow
next week	next month	next year	next Sunday
in a few minutes	in a few hours	in a week	in a month

▶ **3. Pronunciation**

In natural, reduced speech, **going to** is pronounced /gonna/.

Do **not** write *gonna*.

15 Going on Vacation

Dictionary: Vacation Destinations and Plans

A. Listen and repeat. Then, label the pictures.

an amusement park	a beach	a historic site	a play
an art museum	a cabin	a lake	a sporting event
an aquarium	a carnival	a national park	a zoo

1. _____

2. _____

3. _____

4. _____

5. _____

6. _____

7. _____

8. _____

9. _____

10. _____

11. _____

12. _____

B. Listen and repeat. Then, label the pictures.

rent a car	sunbathe	take a tour
rent a house	take pictures	visit a city

1. _____ 2. _____ 3. _____

4. _____ 5. _____ 6. _____

 C. Verbs with *go*. Listen and repeat. Then, label the pictures.

go skiing
go camping
go surfing
go fishing
go hiking

1. _____ 2. _____

3. _____ 4. _____ 5. _____

Active Grammar: Future Tense Questions

A. Read and check (✓). Which are popular vacation places and activities in your country?

☐ resorts	☐ skiing
☐ carnivals	☐ camping
☐ museums	☐ dancing
☐ historic sites	☐ going to sporting events
☐ an aquarium	☐ visiting cities
☐ an amusement park	☐ surfing
☐ mountains	☐ fishing

Discuss the checked items (✓) with a partner.

B. What can you do in your state?

My state is _____.
name of your state

1. I can _____ in / at _____.
   action place / city / location

2. I can _____ in / at _____.
   action place / city / location

3. I can _____ in / at _____.
   place / city / location

4. I can _____ in / at _____.

5. I can _____ in / at _____.

6. In my state, I can't _____.
   action

7. In my state, I can't _____.
   action

8. In my state, I can't _____.

9. In my state, I can't _____.

 *Yes/No Questions*

A. Read the chart. Look at the picture.

Am	I		
Are	we you they	going to	visit a museum? see an aquarium? swim in a lake? go to a carnival?
Is	she he it		

Yes, they are.
No, they aren't.

Yes, he is.
No, he isn't.

Ben   Belinda

B. Listen and complete.

1. Are Ben and Belinda _____ *going to visit* _____ their grandparents?

2. Are they _____ alone?

3. Are they _____ by train?

4. Are they _____ in a hotel?

5. Are they _____ at the beach?

6. Are they _____ hiking?

7. _____ Ben _____ ?

8. _____ Belinda _____ in the lake?

 Practice asking and answering the questions with a partner.

C. Look at the picture. Read and answer the questions.

Yes, he is.
No, he isn't.

1. Is José going to stay at a lake?
2. Is he going to stay a week?
3. Is he going to travel alone?
4. Is he going to travel by public transportation?
5. Is he going to go fishing?
6. Is he going to stay in a hotel?

D. Look at the picture. Read and complete.

| go | rent | see | stay | visit |

1. ___Are___ Donna and Debbie ___going to go___ to Boston?
2. _____ they _____ two weeks?
3. _____ they _____ at a hotel?
4. _____ they _____ their cousins?
5. _____ they _____ a car?
6. _____ they _____ a historic site?

 Practice asking and answering the questions with a partner.

Wh- Questions

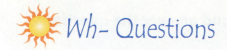

A. Listen and complete.

1. _____*Who*_____ is going to _____*go*_____ on a honeymoon?

2. _____ are _____ going to _____?

3. _____ are _____ going to _____?

4. _____ are _____ going to _____?

5. _____ are _____ going to _____?

6. _____ are _____ going to _____?

7. _____ are _____ going to _____

   during the day?

8. _____ are _____ going to _____

   in the evening?

 B. Ask and answer the questions with a partner.

C. Look at the information in the chart below. Ask and answer the questions with a partner.

Where are they going?
Where . . . ?
What . . . ?

They're going to Colorado.
They're going to stay at a cabin.
They're going to go hiking and . . .

Who	The Lee Family	Jim and Linda	Makiko
Where	A cabin in the mountains of Colorado	A nice hotel in Hawaii	Her sister's house in Washington, D.C.
What	go hiking go swimming go fishing	go sunbathing go swimming ride a boat	visit the museums see the zoo take a lot of pictures

 D. Answer the questions, using a time expression.

tomorrow	next week	later	in (year)
this weekend	next month		in (month)
	next summer		
	next year		

1. When are you going to take a vacation?   I'm going to take a vacation . . .

2. When are you going to visit your country?   I'm going to visit my country . . .

3. When is your teacher going to give a test?   My teacher's going to give a test . . .

4. When is this class going to finish?   This class is going to finish . . .

5. When are you going to see your family?   I'm going to see them . . .

6. When are you going to see a movie?

7. When are you going to visit a new city?

8. When are you going to have a day off?

Questions with /gonna/

 A. Pronunciation: Questions with /gonna/. Listen and repeat.

1. Are you going to leave tomorrow?
2. Is she going to visit her family?
3. Is he going to take the bus?
4. Are they going to stay at a hotel?
5. Is it going to take a long time?

6. How are you going to get there?
7. How much are we going to pay?
8. Who is going to go with you?
9. What are you going to do there?
10. When is she going to return?

Practice the questions with a partner.

 ## Working Together: Student to Student

A. STUDENT A: Turn to page 222.

STUDENT B: Listen to Student A. Answer questions 1 to 4. Then, read questions 5 to 8. Student A will answer.

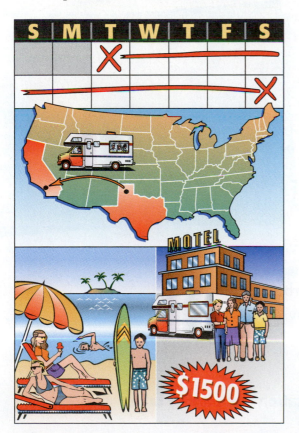

1. a. Yes
   b. No
2. a. Yes
   b. No
3. a. 11 days
   b. Next week
   c. By air
4. a. The grandparents
   b. The Gardner Family
   c. The children
5. Are they going to go to the beach?
6. Are they going to stay at a hotel?
7. How much are they going to spend?
8. When are they going to return?

B. STUDENT A: Read questions 1 to 4. Student B will answer. Then, listen and answer questions 5 to 8.

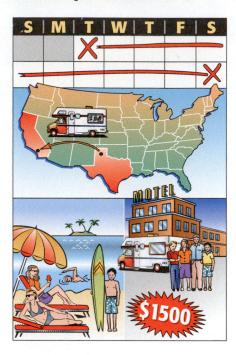

1. Are they going to leave on Thursday?
2. Are they going to go to Texas?
3. How long are they going to stay?
4. Who's going to go on vacation?
5. a. Yes
   b. No
6. a. Yes
   b. No
7. a. 12 days
   b. $1,500
   c. By airplane
8. a. Tomorrow
   b. 11 days
   c. Next week

C. Read and practice.

A: Are you going to take a vacation next summer?

B: Yes, I am.

A: Where are you going to go?

B: My family and I are going to the beach.

A: The beach? Where are you going to stay?

B: We're going to rent a house.

A: What are you going to do there?

B: We're going to go swimming, we're going to visit friends, and we're going to barbecue every day.

A: How long are you going to stay?

B: We're going to stay for a week.

A: Have a good trip.

 D. Write a conversation about a vacation you plan to take.

E. Travel poster. Make a travel poster of your native country or the city where you live now. Use the travel poster here as an example. You can add a simple map of your country, post cards, or other information to make your poster interesting. Present your poster to the class.

Enjoy Beautiful _____ **on Your Next Vacation!**

Spend time at _____.
                        (park)

Tour _____.
                  (historic site)

Relax in the sun on our beautiful beaches in _____ on the
_____.
    (body of water)   (city/town)

See the exhibits at _____.
                              (museum)

Enjoy the _____.
                  (carnival)

Relax in your room at the _____.
                                          (hotel)

Taste delicious _____ food, such as _____
                        (nationality)

and _____.

At night, dance to _____ music at _____
club.

Come to _____!
                (country)

The Big Picture: Vacation Plans

A. Write the names of these cities on the map of the United States.

Chicago, Illinois	Denver, Colorado	Cincinnati, Ohio
Boston, Massachusetts	New York, New York	New Orleans, Louisiana

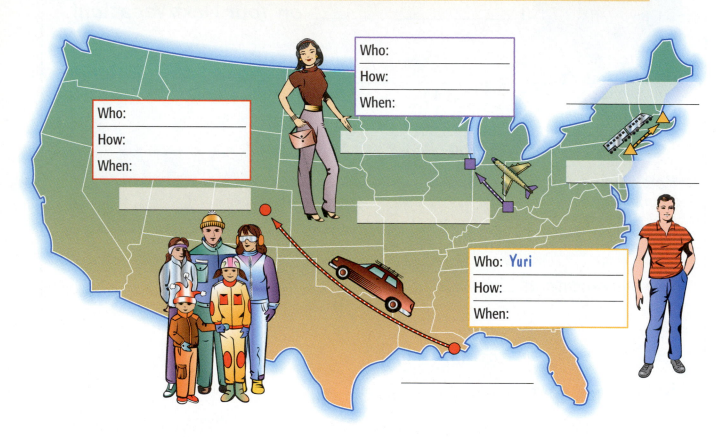

Who: _____
How: _____
When: _____

Who: _____
How: _____
When: _____

Who: **Yuri** _____
How: _____
When: _____

B. Listen and fill in the information on the map.

C. Read and ⬭circle.

1.	Yuri lives in Boston.	Yes	No
2.	He is going to leave on Friday.	Yes	No
3.	He is going to visit his brother.	Yes	No
4.	Lisa is going to fly to Chicago.	Yes	No
5.	She is only going to stay for the weekend.	Yes	No
6.	The Greccos are going to drive to Cincinnati.	Yes	No
7.	They are going to take a winter vacation.	Yes	No

D. Who questions. Read and check (✓) the answers.

Question	Yuri	Lisa	The Greccos
1. Who's going to travel by train?			
2. Who's going to stay for a week?			
3. Who's going to visit a relative?			
4. Who's going to play a sport?			
5. Who's going to go to the mountains?			
6. Who's going to visit museums?			
7. Who's going to spend time on the road?			

E. Match each question with the correct answer.

1. Where is Lisa going to go?
2. Is she going to drive?
3. Where is she going to stay?
4. What is she going to do ?
5. Is Yuri going to take the train?
6. Where is Yuri going to stay?
7. What is he going to do in Boston?

a. She's going to stay at her sister's apartment.
b. Yes, he is.
c. He's going to stay at a downtown hotel.
d. She's going to Chicago.
e. He's going to see the aquarium.
f. No, she isn't.
g. She's going to visit museums, the zoo, and have an interview.

F. Complete each question.

1. Where _____ Yuri _____ for his vacation?
2. Who _____ Yuri _____ dinner with?
3. Why _____ Lisa _____ Chicago?
4. Where _____ Lisa _____ a job interview?
5. How _____ the Greccos _____?
6. How long _____ they _____?

go
travel
eat
visit
have
stay

Reading: An Alaskan Vacation

A. Before You Read. Read the vocabulary and look at the pictures.

river rafting   wild animals   glaciers   lodge   whales

bears   moose   caribou   salmon

It is impossible to see all of Alaska in one visit. Alaska is a very large state, and it has many natural wonders. There are many things to see and to do in Alaska, so most people only choose three or four places to visit.

Fly to Anchorage, the state's largest city. From there, rent a car and drive to the Kenai Peninsula. The Kenai River offers the best salmon fishing in the world. You can catch a thirty- to forty-pound salmon. The largest salmon ever caught in this river was 98 pounds. If you like water, and if you like something fast and exciting, you can go river rafting on the Kenai River.

Drive back to Anchorage and buy a ticket for your trip on the Alaska Railroad to Denali National Park. This eight-hour ride passes beautiful mountains, rivers, and valleys. The only way to see Denali is in a park bus. Make a reservation for the bus. From the bus, you can see the interesting, wild land of Alaska. Look carefully for bears, moose, and caribou. If it is a clear day, you will see Mt. McKinley, the highest mountain in the United States. You can camp in the park or stay a few nights in one of the few lodges inside the park. Then, take a bus back to Anchorage.

Finally, fly to Juneau, the state capital. The city is beautiful, and it is popular to take a day trip on Mendenhall Glacier. You will want to spend most of your time on the water. Many small companies offer trips in the waters near Juneau. You can stay from one day to one week. You can watch for whales, view the wildlife, or look at the giant

glaciers. If you choose a smaller boat, you can go to a beach for a picnic lunch, fish from the boat, or walk up to a glacier.

A visit to Alaska takes a lot of planning. Visitors need to make reservations for flights, hotels, and cruises before they arrive. Remember to bring your camera and extra film. You will want to record your many memories of this wild, beautiful state.

B. After You Read.

1. This article describes three areas to visit in Alaska. <u>Underline</u> these three areas. Find these three areas on the map. What can you do at each location?

2. What's the best way to travel in Alaska?

3. Complete the chart below. Check (✓) a good place for each activity.

	Kenai	Denali	Juneau
1. I can view wild animals.			
2. I can fish.			
3. I can watch for whales.			
4. I can take great pictures.			
5. I can see the largest mountain in the U.S.			
6. I can see glaciers.			
7. I can take a river rafting trip.			

Writing Our Stories: My Next Vacation

A. Read these topics. Choose one. Write in your notebook.

1. **My next vacation.** Where are you going to go on your next vacation? How are you going to get there? How long are you going to stay? What are you going to do there? What can a tourist do and see in each place?

2. **A visit to my country.** A tourist is going to visit your country. Describe three places to visit.

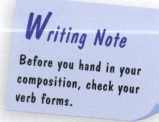

Writing Note

Before you hand in your composition, check your verb forms.

Practicing on Your Own

A. Complete with the question word.

How	What	Who	Why	When	Where	How many	How long

1. _____ is she going to do there?   She's going to ski.

2. _____ is he going to stay?   One week.

3. _____ is it going to take?   Three hours.

4. _____ are you going to return?   Next Sunday.

5. _____ is going to meet you there?   My sister is.

6. _____ are they going to go there?   Because the weather is good there.

7. _____ is he going to get there?   He's going to drive.

8. _____ cities are you going to visit?   Four.

9. _____ is she going to stay?   At her friend's house.

B. Put the words in the questions in the correct order. Then, answer the questions.

1. what / you / do / tonight / are / going to

   _____?

2. when / you / study / going to / are

   _____?

3. going to / what time / the students / go / home / are

   _____?

4. your country / going to / you / when / are / visit

   _____?

5. going to / the teacher / give / a test / tomorrow / is

   _____?

Looking at a Top Ten List: Summer Vacations

A. Where are Americans going to go on summer vacations? Read the list of the top ten places.

1. Go to a beach or a lake
2. Visit friends and relatives
3. Visit a city
4. Attend a cultural event
5. Visit a historic place
6. Go fishing
7. Go camping, hiking, or climbing
8. Visit a theme park such as Disneyland
9. Travel in an RV (Recreational Vehicle)
10. Stay in a resort

(Source: Travel Industry Association of America)

1. Are you going to take a vacation next summer?
2. Which of the ten activities are you going to do? Are you going to do something that is not on the list?
3. Survey your classmates. Make a top ten list. Ask, "What are you going to do next summer?"

Grammar Summary

▶ **1. Yes/No questions**

Am I going to visit a friend?	Yes, you are.	No, you're not.	No, you aren't.
Are you going to see your relatives?	Yes, I am.	No, I'm not.	
Is he going to take the train?	Yes, he is.	No, he's not	No, he isn't.
Is she going to rent a car?	Yes, she is.	No, she's not.	No, she isn't.
Are we going to stay at a hotel?	Yes, we are.	No, we're not.	No, we aren't.
Are they going to drive?	Yes, they are.	No, they're not.	No, they aren't.

▶ **2. Wh- questions**

When am I going to visit?	Next week.
What are you going to do there?	I'm going to go hiking and swimming.
How long is she going to stay?	She's going to stay for 10 days.
How long is it going to take?	It's going to take three hours.
How are we going to get there?	By train.
Why are they going to go there?	Because it's not expensive.
Who is going to pay for the tickets?	My parents are.

Unit 1: Nice to Meet You

Page 7

C. Listen and complete the registration form.

A: I need some information for the registration form. What's your first name?

B: Boris.

A: And your last name?

B: Galkin.

A: Please spell that.

B: Galkin—G-A-L-K-I-N.

A: What's your address?

B: 514 North Avenue.

A: And the city?

B: Richmond.

A: What's your zip code?

B: 23223

A: And what's your telephone number?

B: 555-7833.

A: 555-7833?

B: Yes.

A: And what country are you from, Boris?

B: I'm from Russia.

Page 12

The Big Picture: Registering for Class

A. Listen and complete the form.

Akiko is a new student at Miami Adult School. She's in the office now. She's registering for class.

A: What is your first name?

B: My first name is Akiko.

A: A-K-I-K-O?

B: Yes.

A: And your last name?

B: Tanaka.

A: Please spell that.

B: T-A-N-A-K-A

A: What's your address?

B: 337 Bay Avenue.

A: And the city?

B: Kendall.

A: What's your zip code?

B: 33156.

A: What's your telephone number?

B: 555-4739

A: 555-4739?

B: Yes.

A: What's your birth date?

B: Birth date?

A: Yes, your birth date.

B: I don't understand birth date.

A: Your date of birth, the day you were born, maybe 1979 or 1980.

B: Oh! I understand! March 4, 1980.

A: And what country are you from?

B: I'm from Japan.

A: Thank you, Akiko. You are in Miss Bayard's class. That's Room 217.

B: Excuse me?

A: You are in Room 217. That's two-one-seven, 217. It's upstairs.
Go up those stairs to Room 217. Give this paper to Miss Bayard.

B: OK. Thank you.

Page 13

C. Listen and write the questions.

1. What's your name?
2. What's your address?
3. What's your telephone number?
4. What's your birth date?
5. What country are you from?

Unit 2: My Classmates

Page 26

The Big Picture: A New Student

B. Listen to the conversation between Adam and Ben. Then, listen to the questions and circle the correct answers.

Two students are standing in line in the college bookstore.

Adam: Are you buying a dictionary?

Ben: Yes, I am.

Adam: You know, I think you're in my class, English 2?

Ben: With Mr. Baxter?

Adam: Yes. At 9:00. In Room 312.

Ben: Yeah. We are in the same class.

Adam: My name is Adam.

Ben: Hi, Adam. My name is Ben.

Adam: Hi, Ben. Are you a new student?

Ben: Yes. This is my first week at school.

Adam: This is my second year here. What country are you from?

Ben: I'm from India. How about you?

Adam: I'm from Poland. What classes are you taking?

Ben: English, and writing, and math. How about you?

Adam: The same. And I have a computer class. I'm going to the cafeteria for a sandwich. Want to come?

Ben: Sure. I'd like a soda.

1. Where are Adam and Ben?
2. What is Ben buying?
3. Who is their teacher?
4. Where is their class?
5. Is Adam a new student?
6. Is Adam from Poland or from India?
7. Where are they going?

Unit 3: At School

Page 35

C. Pronunciation: Final s. Listen and circle.

1. backpack
2. bookcases
3. clocks
4. teacher
5. tape recorders
6. women
7. notebook
8. students
9. examinations
10. table
11. classes
12. eraser
13. man
14. pencils
15. map
16. dictionaries
17. desks
18. computer

Page 36

C. Listen and circle.

1. A: What time is it?
   B: It's three–oh five.
2. A: What time is it?
   B: It's four forty.
3. A: What time is it?
   B: It's twelve twenty.
4. A: What time is it?
   B: It's one fifty-five.
5. A: What time is it?
   B: It's two ten.
6. A: What time is it?
   B: It's ten fifteen.

Page 40

The Big Picture: My New Classroom

B. Listen and look at the pictures.

I'm a teacher in an adult school. I teach math at night. My class meets every Tuesday and Thursday from 7:00 to 9:00. There are 15 students in my class. This is a picture of my classroom in September, 2000. Look at it. It's depressing, isn't it? There are no windows. There's no desk for me—only a very small table. I put my backpack on the floor. The room is ugly. The paint on the walls is old. There's a clock, but the clock's broken. There are many chairs in this small room, so the students are not comfortable. It's difficult for them to study in this room.

Now, look at this picture. This is a picture of my new room. It's great. The room is clean and bright. Now I have a big window. There are two maps on the wall: one of the United States and one of the world. There's one big bookcase, and there's a large chalkboard to write on. There are no desks for the students because now we have three long tables. Five students can sit at each table. And there's a computer and a printer. I really like my new classroom.

Page 41

C. Listen and circle.

1. There's one bookcase.
2. There are two maps.
3. There is a small table for the teacher.
4. There are no windows.
5. There's a computer.
6. There's a small chalkboard.
7. There's a big desk for the teacher.
8. There are no desks.

Unit 4: The Family

Page 47

C. Listen and complete.

1. Susan is Rich's **wife.**
2. Rich is Susan's **husband.**
3. Caroline is Rich and Susan's **daughter.**
4. Matt is Rich and Susan's **son.**
5. Caroline is Matt's **sister.**
6. Susan and Rich are Caroline and Matt's **parents.**
7. Caroline and Matt are Susan and Rich's **children.**

Page 48

B. Listen and complete, using *she* or *her*, *he* or *his*, and *they* or *their*.

This is my little sister.
1. **Her** name is Maria.
2. **She**'s sixteen years old today, but **her** birthday is next week.
3. **Her** eyes are brown and **her** hair is long.
4. **She**'s in tenth grade.

This is my brother.
5. **His** name is David.
6. **He**'s nineteen years old, and **he**'s in college.
7. **His** birthday is on October 2nd.
8. **He**'s a baseball player.

This is my brother, Steve, and his wife, Sue.
9. **They**'re married and **they** live in Florida.
10. **Their** house is in Miami.
11. **They** have two children. **Their** names are Brian and Kevin.

Page 52

B. Listen and complete.
1. What's **her** name?
2. What's **his** name?
3. What's **your** address?
4. What's **her** address?
5. What's **your** job?
6. What's **his** job?

Page 54

The Big Picture: A Family Reunion
B. Listen and label the family members.

A: Oh, Victoria, this is a great picture. Is this your family?
B: Yes, it is. It's our family reunion at the park.
A: Are these your children?
B: Yes, I have three daughters and a son: Barbara, Betty, Benita, and that's Bobby next to the tree. And that's my daughter-in-law, Julia. She's talking with my daughters.
A: Where's your husband?
B: There he is. That's Frank over there, sitting under the tree. He's with Bobby, of course.
A: Oh, look at the babies. They're so cute. Are they your grandchildren?
B: Yes, those are my grandbabies. That's Bobby, Jr. He's two. And that's Erika. She's four. They're Bobby and Julia's children.
A: Are those your grandchildren, too?
B: Yes, they're Benita's children. They're twins. That's Victor and Valerie.
A: Well, this is a wonderful picture. Did you have a good time?
B: We had a wonderful time.

Unit 5: Home and Neighborhood

Page 61

C. Listen and repeat.

in	between	in front of
on	under	in back of / behind
next to	over	

1. The cat is in the basket.
2. The cat is on the TV.
3. The cat is next to the chair.
4. The cat is between the sofa and the chair.
5. The cat is under the coffee table.
6. The cat is over the sofa.
7. The cat is in front of the refrigerator.
8. The cat is in back of the chair.
   The cat is in behind the chair.

Page 62

A. Bob's room is always a mess. He's asking his mother about each item. Listen and write the number of each location.

a. **A:** Mom, where's my telephone?
   B: I think it's under your bed.

b. **A:** Mom, where's my wallet?
   B: I think it's on your desk, next to your computer.

c. **A:** Mom, where are my keys?
   B: I think they're on your night table.

d. **A:** Mom, where's my soccer ball?
   B: Look in your closet.

e. **A:** Mom, where's my backpack?
   B: I think it's in front of your dresser.

f. **A:** Mom, where is my other sneaker?
   B: Look under your desk.

Page 70

The Big Picture: Pine Street

B. Listen to the story. Then, read and circle.

My name is Magda Santos. I live in an apartment building on Pine Street between Second Street and Third Street. My address is 232 Pine Street, Apartment 4G. My apartment is on the fourth floor. I live in a two-bedroom apartment with my husband and my two daughters. My sister lives in the next building, at 234 Pine Street. She's in Apartment 3A. I like my apartment and my neighborhood.

The elementary school is very near my building, it's across the street, on the corner of Pine Street and Third Street. My daughters can walk to school. There's a small park next to the school. My daughters play there on Saturday and Sunday. The grocery store is on the corner of Pine and Third Street. There's a coffee shop across the street from our apartment buildings. Sometimes my sister and I get a cup of coffee and sit and talk. My building doesn't have a laundry room, but that isn't a problem. There is a laundromat next to our apartment building. There are many restaurants in the neighborhood—Mexican, Italian, Chinese, and Indian. I like to try different food. There's a parking lot in back of the apartment buildings. Each apartment has only one space.

My husband takes the bus to work. The bus stop is on the corner of Pine and Second Street, in front of the laundromat. Sometimes, Pine Street is busy and noisy, and there is a lot of traffic, but that's OK. Everything is convenient, and the neighbors are friendly.

Page 71

E. Listen and respond to each statement. Use *That's good* or *That's too bad*.

1. The apartment is large.
2. The neighborhood is noisy.
3. The neighbors are friendly.
4. The school is near my apartment building.
5. My sister lives in the next building.
6. The traffic is heavy.
7. The bus stop is on the corner.
8. There's no laundry room in the building.
9. The laundromat is next to my building.
10. Each apartment has only one parking space.

Unit 6: A Typical Day

Page 83

A. Pronunciation: Final *s*. Listen and repeat.

/ s /	/ z /	/ əs /
wakes	drives	fixes
walks	arrives	relaxes
takes	does	washes
drinks	goes	brushes
likes	knows	watches
eats	plays	
gets	wears	
sleeps		
shops		

Page 86

The Big Picture: A Daily Schedule

A. Listen to Susan's and Peter's schedules. Write the correct times on each clock. Then, talk about their schedules.

Susan and Peter have busy schedules during the week. At 6:00, the alarm rings, and Susan and Peter wake up. Susan exercises for half an hour—she runs from 6:30 to 7:00. Peter takes a shower and gets dressed. At 7:30, they are in the kitchen. Susan and Peter eat breakfast. Susan eats yogurt, fruit, and drinks water. Peter eats toast and eggs. He always drinks coffee. At 8:00, they leave for work. Peter drives to work and Susan walks. Susan works in an office. She's a secretary. Peter works for a construction company. They both work from 9:00 to 5:00. They eat dinner together at 6:00. At 7:00, they go to classes at the community college. They have classes from 7:00 to 9:00 two times a week. From 9:30 to 11:00, they relax. Susan likes to read. Peter usually watches TV. At 11:00, they go to bed.

Unit 7: Airport Jobs

Page 94

A. Listen and complete the information about Alberto's job.

A: Alberto, where do you work?
B: I work at Atlanta Airport.
A: What do you do?
B: I'm a mechanic. I repair passenger planes and cargo planes.
A: What's your schedule?
B: I work from Wednesday to Sunday, from 5 A.M. to 1 P.M.
A: You get up early! Do you work overtime?
B: Oh, yes. I put in lots of overtime.
A: Do you wear a uniform?
B: Yes, we all wear company uniform: blue pants and a blue shirt.
A: Do you like your job?
B: Yes, I do. I like it a lot.

Page 95

F. Listen and complete. Then, answer the questions.

1. Where does Ellen work?
2. What does she do?
3. What airline does she work for?
4. What's her schedule?
5. Does she work on weekends?
6. What route does she fly?
7. Does she like her job?

Page 99

C. Listen and write the salary and benefits.

Karina

Manager:	Your salary is $8 an hour. Overtime pay is $10 an hour.
Karina:	What are the benefits?
Manager:	You have medical benefits after six months. You have three sick days and one week vacation the first year.

Mohammed

Mohammed:	What is the salary?
Manager:	The salary is $6 an hour plus tips.
Mohammed:	And the benefits?
Manager:	For part-time employees, there are no benefits.

Li-Ping

Manager:	The starting salary is $9 an hour.
Li-Ping:	And the overtime pay?
Manager:	The overtime pay is the same, $9 an hour.
Li-Ping:	Are there medical benefits?
Manager:	Yes, there are medical benefits and a prescription plan. You have two sick days and two weeks' vacation.

Juan

Manager:	The salary is $14 an hour. After six months, it's $16 an hour.
Juan:	And the benefits?
Manager:	We have a good benefit package here. There's medical and dental and prescription. You have five sick days and two weeks' vacation the first year. The second year, you have three weeks' vacation.

Page 101

D. Pronunciation: *Does he/Does she.* Listen and complete.

1. Does **she** work full time?
2. Does **he** work on weekends?
3. Does **she** use a computer at work?
4. Does **he** speak English at work?
5. Does **he** need a driver's license?
6. Does **she** get good benefits?
7. Does **he** have a dental plan?

Page 102

The Big Picture: The Interview

A. Listen: Mr. Chan is in the personnel office of a major airport. He is applying for a position as an electric cart driver. An electric cart driver assists elderly passengers or passengers who need assistance.

A:	Good morning, Mr. Chan. I'm Ms. Ross.
B:	Good morning, Ms. Ross.
A:	Mr. Chan, I have your application in front of me. I see that you work at the airport now. You are a parking lot attendant.
B:	Yes, Ms. Ross. I collect tolls. Sometimes I help passengers find their cars.
A:	And why are you interested in a job as an electric cart driver?
B:	I started to work at the airport two years ago. I didn't speak much English. Now, I speak English much better. This job is a promotion for me. I make eight dollars an hour now. The salary for this job is one dollar more an hour.
A:	Do you have a driver's license?
B:	Yes.
A:	Do you have any tickets? Any accidents?
B:	No, I don't. I have a clean driving record.

A: You have a good letter of recommendation from your supervisor. When are you available to work?

B: I can work any hours.

A: Many of the passengers who need assistance are elderly. Do you have any experience with older people?

B: Yes. My grandfather is in a wheelchair. I often help him. I'm a friendly person and comfortable with everyone.

A: Do you have any questions?

B: Do I receive the same benefits?

A: You still get medical benefits. But in this job you also have a prescription plan. Your vacation is the same, two weeks. Anything else?

B: No, that's all.

A: I'm going to interview two more applicants. I will call you on Friday about the position.

B: Thank you for the interview, Ms. Ross.

Unit 8: A College Campus

Page 109

A. Listen and complete with *is* or *are* and a quantity expression.

1. There **are a few** benches outside.
2. There **are many** students outside the building.
3. There **is a** statue in front of the building.
4. There **are several** garbage cans outside.
5. There **is a** pay telephone next to the building.
6. There **isn't a** bus at the bus stop.
7. There **are a lot of** cars in the parking lot.
8. There **aren't any** students at the bus stop.

Page 112

I. Listen and complete these sentences.

1. **There are** many cars on campus.
2. **They are** in the parking lot.
3. **There aren't** any buses.
4. **They aren't** on the bus.
5. **There aren't** any students in the cafeteria.
6. **They are** in class.
7. **There are** many students in the gym.
8. **They aren't** in the pool.

Page 116

The Big Picture: Campus Information

A. Listen and write the symbol for each location on the map above.

Conversation 1

A: I love tennis. Are there any courts on campus?

B: Yes. There are four tennis courts in back of the gym.

Conversation 2

A: I need some cash. Is there an ATM machine on campus?

B: Yes, there are several. I know that there's one in the Student Center and there's another one in the bookstore.

A: Thanks.

Conversation 3

A: Are there any pay telephones on campus?

B: Not many. Most students have cell phones. I think there's one in the Student Center.

Conversation 4

A: This parking lot is for faculty. Where are the student parking lots?

B: There are some student parking lots in back of the dorms.
And there's a big student parking lot in back of the theater.

Conversation 5

A: I'm looking for a mailbox.

B: There's one in front of the library. And there's
a small post office in the Student Center.

Conversation 6

A: Is there a bus stop around here?

B: Yes, there's one down the street, in front of the Administration Building.

Unit 9: At Work

Page 132

The Big Picture: Inspection at the Factory

B. Listen and write the names of the employees.

It's a very hot summer day. The factory is very busy. Today is a bad day for the factory and for the manager. The manager, Mr. Brooks, is listening to the inspector, Mr. DiMauro. There are many problems in the factory. Mr. DiMauro has a long list of safety violations. Victor is smoking in a non-smoking area. Vladimir is carrying a heavy box. He isn't wearing work boots. He's wearing sandals. Gloria and Anna are working in the cafeteria. Gloria is wearing a hairnet, but Anna isn't. Anna is wearing gloves, but Gloria isn't. Joseph and Frank are working in the hard-hat area, but they aren't following the factory's safety rules. They aren't wearing their hard hats. Louise is six months pregnant and she is still standing up. She's tired. She needs to sit down. Luis and Carmen are working together. Luis is wearing safety glasses, but Carmen isn't. Finally, the fire door is open. Mr. Brooks looks very upset. He will have to pay a big fine.

Unit 10: Fast Food

Page 141

A. Listen and complete with the question words.

1. **What** are they eating?
2. **What** is Mary eating?
3. **Where** are they eating breakfast?
4. **What** is Vera drinking?
5. **How many** donuts is Vera eating?
6. **Who** is drinking coffee?
7. **What kind of** coffee is Patricia drinking?
8. **Why** are they smiling?

Page 146

The Big Picture: Coffee to Go

B. Listen and label the people in the picture.

It's early in the morning at Coffee to Go. Kate is working behind the counter. She's at the cash register. She's taking another order. She's tired because she's working overtime again. Sherri is standing in front of the counter. She is taking her coffee. Sherri is on her way to work. Pete's another employee behind the counter. He's pouring a large coffee for a customer. Jess is standing behind Sherri. He always orders the same thing: a large coffee and two donuts. He is giving his order to Kate, but Pete is already pouring Jess a large coffee. Jess comes to Coffee to Go every weekday morning. His office is across the street. Standing at the table is Mr. Lopez. He's putting sugar in his coffee. He likes his coffee dark and sweet. Sitting at a table are three regular customers: Mary, Vera, and Patricia. They're senior citizens, and they visit Coffee to Go three times a week after they take a walk in the park. They like to have breakfast together after their walk. Mary is drinking a cup of tea and eating eggs and a bagel. Vera is eating two donuts and drinking some orange juice. Patricia is eating a donut and is drinking a cup of decaf coffee. They're talking and smiling. It's a good morning for them. But, it's not a good morning for Scott. He is a good worker, but was late again. Harry, his manager, is talking to him. Scott is wiping a table and listening to Harry. Harry is angry. He is telling Scott that he must not be late again. Harry is telling Scott to stay late today.

Unit 11: Food Shopping

Page 155

A. Listen to this couple make a shopping list. Check the items they need.

1. **A:** Do we need any milk?
   B: No, we don't need any milk.
2. **A:** Do we need hot dogs?
   B: Yes, we need some hot dogs.
3. **A:** Do we need any cheese?
   B: Yes, we need some cheese.
4. **A:** How about lettuce? Do we need any lettuce for the salad?
   B: Yes, we do. I don't see any in here. And please get a tomato and a cucumber.
5. **A:** Do we have any mayonnaise?
   B: Yes, we have some. We don't need any.
6. **A:** Do we need eggs?
   B: No, we have six, seven, eight eggs. We don't need any.
7. **A:** Do we have any dessert?
   B: Yes. Let's have an apple pie tonight. But, we don't need any cookies. We have a lot of cookies.

Page 162

The Big Picture: The Shopping List

B. Listen. This couple needs some food at the supermarket. Circle the items they need. Cross out the items they don't need.

M: What do we need at the store?
W: Not too much. I went to the store a few days ago. We need fruit—apples, bananas, but we don't need any oranges. There are four in the refrigerator. And we have a pineapple, too.
M: How about milk and juice?
W: Milk, yes. We always need milk. But we have orange juice and apple juice.
M: What about meat?
W: Get some chicken and some pork chops. We don't need any beef.
M: Okay.
W: There's a sale on paper products. Get about four rolls of toilet paper and two boxes of tissues. But we don't need any paper towels.
M: Any cereal?
W: Let's see. There are three boxes in the cabinet. But we need a large box of rice and some spaghetti.
M: Are there any good coupons in the paper today?
W: I cut out some coupons. There are coupons for coffee and peanut butter.
M: Okay. Anything else?
W: Yes, some fresh vegetables, any kind you like. And pick up some ice cream for the kids.
M: I never forget the ice cream.

Unit 12: Last Weekend

Page 170

A. Listen: Ali's morning. Ali went downtown on Saturday morning. Where did he go first, second, third, etc.? Number the locations from 1 to 8 on the map above.

I always go downtown on Saturday morning. It's the only day I have free all week. So, last Saturday I walked downtown as usual. First, I went to the bank and deposited my paycheck.

Then, I walked across the street to the shoe store. I tried on two or three pairs of sneakers, but I didn't see anything that I liked. Next, I stopped at the post office and mailed a letter to my brother. Then, I walked to the drugstore and picked up a prescription for my wife. Next door at the camera store, I dropped off some film, and I picked up the pictures from my son's birthday party. After that, I rented a movie at the video store for Saturday night. My family always watches a movie on Saturday night. I was a little hungry, so I stopped at the coffee shop and ordered juice, a cup of coffee, and a donut. Then, I walked over to the library. They have a lot of newspapers, and I looked at the Arabic language paper from my country. Also, I finally applied for a library card. That was my last stop and I walked back home.

Page 178

The Big Picture: The Wrong Directions

B. Listen to the story about Paula. Then, answer the questions.

Paula was very excited. She was going to a birthday party. The party was at a friend's house from work.

Paula's friend carefully wrote the directions to the party. Paula didn't know the town where her friend lived, so she left her house early. For 20 minutes she followed the directions carefully and got off at Exit 14. Then, she began to have problems. She couldn't find the street. She drove around and around, and soon she was lost. She stopped and asked people for directions, but no one knew that street. Paula didn't have her cell phone with her. She left it at home on the kitchen table. Finally, she saw a police officer. She stopped and asked for directions. The officer looked at the directions and smiled. "You wanted Exit 15, not Exit 14." He showed Paula how to get back on the highway. She got off at Exit 15 and easily found the house. She was very late! When she walked in, everyone was singing Happy Birthday to her friend. After a few minutes, Paula relaxed and began to enjoy the party.

Unit 13: Growing Up

Page 187

D. Listen and complete the questions. Then, write the answers.
1. Did Alex **come to the U.S.** in **1985?**
2. Did Alex **move** to New York in **1996?**
3. Did Alex **change jobs** in 1998?
4. Did Alex **fall in love** with Lena in **2000?**
5. Did they **have a baby** in **2002?**

Page 187

A. Listen and answer.

Paul

Hi, I'm Paul. I grew up in New Jersey. After college, I got a job at a bank in New York City. I didn't like my job, so I changed jobs. I found a job at a computer company.

Marta

Hi, I'm Marta. I grew up in El Salvador. I went to nursing school there and then, last year, I moved to the United States. I got a job at a hospital in New Jersey.

Page 194

The Big Picture: Growing Up

A. Listen and look at the pictures.

Hi, my name is Oscar Vega. I'm 21 years old, and I'm a student here at The University of Texas. I was born in a small town in Mexico. I started school when I was 6 years old. Let's see, what can I remember? One summer, when I was 7, I fell off my bicycle and broke my arm. When I was in second grade, I got chicken pox. My brothers and sister got chicken pox, too. And when I was a kid, I played soccer all the time—before school, after school, and on weekends. I made the school team. When I was 12, our team won a championship and I got a trophy. Then, when I was 14, I moved to the United States with my parents. We moved here to Dallas, Texas. I started high school here in Dallas, but I didn't like it at first. I didn't know anyone, and I wasn't on the soccer team. But, I knew a little English and I learned it fast. The year I turned 16 was great for me. My father taught me how to drive, and I got my license. When I was 17, I found my first job—it was at a pizza place. After I graduated from high school, I started college. I'm still working at the pizza place, and now I'm the assistant manager. I'm majoring in business, and working nights and weekends.

C. Listen and circle.

1. Where was Oscar born?
2. How did he break his arm?
3. When did he get chicken pox?
4. When did his team win the soccer championship?
5. Where did Oscar move?
6. How much English did Oscar know?
7. When did he get his first job?
8. Who taught him how to drive?

Unit 14: Weekend Plans

Page 202

A. Listen and complete.

1. **He's going to do** the laundry.
2. **She's going to wash** the dishes.
3. **I'm going to vacuum** the carpet.
4. **We're going to celebrate** a birthday.
5. **They're going to play** volleyball.
6. **I'm going to do** my homework.

Page 204

F. Listen and complete.

1. **I'm going to wash** my car tomorrow.
2. The students **are going to study** after class.
3. Some students **aren't going to do** homework tonight.
4. Our teacher **is going to give a test** next week.
5. The school **is going to close** for the holidays.
6. They **aren't going to be** late tomorrow morning.
7. The class **isn't going to end** next month.
8. **I'm going to arrive** at eleven o'clock.

Page 205

F. Listen to Mariana's plans. Circle the activities that she's going to do. Cross out the activities that she's *not* going to do.

I'm going to be very busy this weekend.
First, I'm going to get up early and clean my apartment.
Then, I'm going to do my laundry.
After that, I'm going to study in my apartment. I'm not going to go to the library.
Then, I'm going to go to the supermarket to shop for dinner.
I'm going to cook a special meal for my boyfriend because it's his birthday.
After dinner, my boyfriend and I are going to rent a movie and watch it in my apartment.

Page 208

The Big Picture: A Visitor

B. Look at the picture. Listen to the story.

I'm excited. Tomorrow my mother's going to arrive at the San Francisco Airport. She's coming to visit for two weeks. She's coming from Osaka, Japan. Today I'm going to clean my apartment because she's going to stay with me. Tomorrow, I'm going to pick her up. Then, we're going to drive to my sister's house. We're going to have dinner with all of our friends and family who live in the Bay Area. On Saturday, we're going to sleep late. After a late breakfast, my sister and I are going to show our mother the beautiful city of San Francisco. We're going to take a cable car ride. We're going to visit my favorite park. Then, I'm going to take her to my girlfriend's house. We want to get married next year, so I want my mother to meet her. I hope she likes her.

Unit 15: Going on Vacation

Page 217

B. Listen and complete.
1. Are Ben and Belinda **going to visit** their grandparents?
2. Are they **going to go** alone?
3. Are they **going to travel** by train?
4. Are they **going to stay** in a hotel?
5. Are they **going to stay** at the beach?
6. Are they **going to go** hiking?
7. Is Ben **going to go** fishing?
6. Is Belinda **going to go** swimming in the lake?

Page 219

A. Listen and complete.
1. **Who** is going to **go** on a honeymoon?
2. **Where** are **they** going to **go**?
3. **How** are **they** going to **travel**?
4. **How long** are **they** going to **stay**?
5. **Where** are **they** going to **stay**?
6. **Which cities** are **they** going to **visit**?
7. **What** are **they** going to **do** during the day?
8. **Where** are **they** going to **go** in the evening?

Page 224

The Big Picture: Vacation Plans

B. Listen and fill in the information on the map.

Yuri

Yuri lives in New York and he likes to travel. This weekend, he's going to visit Boston, Massachusetts. He's going to leave Friday afternoon and take the train to Boston. It's a three-hour ride. He's going to stay in a downtown hotel. On Friday night, he's going out to dinner with his sister. On Saturday, he's going to the aquarium. Then, he's going to walk around the historic areas. On Sunday morning, Yuri and his sister are going to visit the Museum of Fine Arts. After lunch, Yuri's going to take the train back home.

Lisa

Lisa and her sister, Linda, are very close, but they don't live in the same city. On Saturday morning, Lisa's going to fly from Cincinnati to Chicago to visit her sister. Lisa's going to stay for a week at her sister's apartment. They're going to visit two museums. They're also going to visit the zoo. Next week, Lisa's going to go to the University of Chicago. She has a job interview there. Next Sunday morning, she's going to fly home.

The Greccos

The Greccos love the snow, and they take a long vacation every winter. This winter, they're going to drive to Denver, Colorado. They're going to spend two weeks away from home. It's a long drive from Louisiana to Colorado, so they're going to spend two days on the road. In Colorado, they're going to stay at a comfortable hotel in the mountains. They're going to go skiing every day. They're going to take a lot of pictures. And, they're going to eat at a different restaurant every night. The Greccos are going to have a great vacation.

Skills Index

Speaking

Ask and answer, 6, 13, 21–22, 24, 38, 52, 62, 67, 68, 82, 84, 96, 99–100, 125, 133, 140, 142, 143–144, 158, 169, 191, 193, 195, 203, 218, 219, 220, 221–222

Conversations, 13, 23, 53, 70, 130, 175–176, 188

Descriptions, 192, 208

Discussions, 86, 131, 132, 145, 146, 207, 216

Interviews, 63, 131

Introductions, 1, 3, 11

Pair practice, 9–11, 21–22, 24, 35, 38, 52, 67, 69, 82, 84, 99–100, 110, 125, 133, 142, 143–144, 171, 186, 204

Pronunciation

Contractions, 5

does he/does she, 101

-ed words, 171

Final *-s*, 35, 83

going to/gonna, 204, 213, 221

I'm, 130

Money amounts, 143

of, 157

or questions, 21

Prepositions, 67

there/they, 112

what's, 52

Repeating, 2–3, 7, 18, 21, 32, 36, 37, 46, 54, 60, 61, 64, 76, 77, 108, 123, 138, 152–153, 168, 184, 185, 200–201, 204, 214–215

Restaurant orders, 144

Technology

Internet, 45, 159

Test-Taking Skills

Circle answers, 6, 9, 10, 24, 26, 28, 35, 36, 38, 41, 42, 63, 70, 88, 94, 95, 96, 104, 112, 118, 132, 134, 148, 150, 154, 160, 187, 194, 208, 224

Matching, 8, 23, 41, 55, 92, 94, 115, 123, 124, 141, 157, 179, 225

Multiple-choice, 26, 36, 84

Sentence completion, 8, 14, 20, 36, 41, 47, 51, 52, 55, 61, 63, 64, 66, 72, 74, 81, 87, 92, 95, 96, 97, 124, 128, 129, 131, 133, 136, 138–139, 141, 147, 155, 156, 163, 164–165, 166, 167, 169, 171, 175, 189, 195, 197, 202, 204, 205, 207, 209, 216, 218, 225, 228

True/false, 28, 38, 42, 70, 88, 94, 95, 103, 104, 112, 114, 118, 130, 169

Topics

College campuses, 108–121

Complaints, 175–176

Countries and cities, 22–23, 23, 25, 28–29

Daily activities, 76–77, 85, 88, 89, 168–174, 177

Downtown, 66–71, 74, 75

Families, 46–57

Food, 152–167

Growing up, 184–189, 192–198

Home, 60–63, 72, 75

Introductions, 1, 3, 11

Neighborhoods, 64–65, 73

Occupations, 50–51, 92–107

Parties, 190–192

Planning weekends, 200–213

Population figures, 31

Registration forms, 7–8, 12

Restaurants, 138–151

Schedules, 78–84, 86–90

School, 37–43, 62

State fairs, 180–181

Teachers, 14

Time, 36

Vacation, 214–229

Writing

Abbreviations, A.M. and P.M., 105

Capitalization, 15, 29, 73, 81, 105

Conversations, 23, 27, 53, 62, 144, 156, 222

Descriptive writing, 19, 24, 26, 29, 43, 149

Interviews, 103

Lists, 11, 40, 148, 154, 155, 156, 157

Proposals, 210

Punctuation

Commas, 119, 190, 211

Questions, 13, 140, 150, 189, 192

Recipes, 165

Registration forms, 7–8, 12, 121

Sentences, 10, 24, 27, 39, 69, 73, 85, 103, 109, 110, 113, 131, 136, 161, 177, 211

Spelling, 137, 172

Stories, 15, 43, 57, 89, 105, 135, 147, 149, 181, 197, 227

Times, 36

Titles, 135

Vocabulary words, 33, 40

Past Tense of Irregular Verbs

be	was / were	leave	left
become	became	lose	lost
begin	began	make	made
bite	bit	meet	met
break	broke	pay	paid
bring	brought	put	put
buy	bought	read	read
catch	caught	ring	rang
choose	chose	run	ran
come	came	say	said
cost	cost	see	saw
do	did	sell	sold
drink	drank	send	sent
drive	drove	sit	sat
eat	ate	sleep	slept
fall	fell	speak	spoke
feel	felt	spend	spent
fight	fought	stand	stood
find	found	steal	stole
fly	flew	swim	swam
forget	forgot	take	took
get	got	teach	taught
give	gave	tell	told
go	went	think	thought
have	had	understand	understood
hear	heard	wake	woke
hold	held	wear	wore
hurt	hurt	write	wrote
know	knew		

Map   245

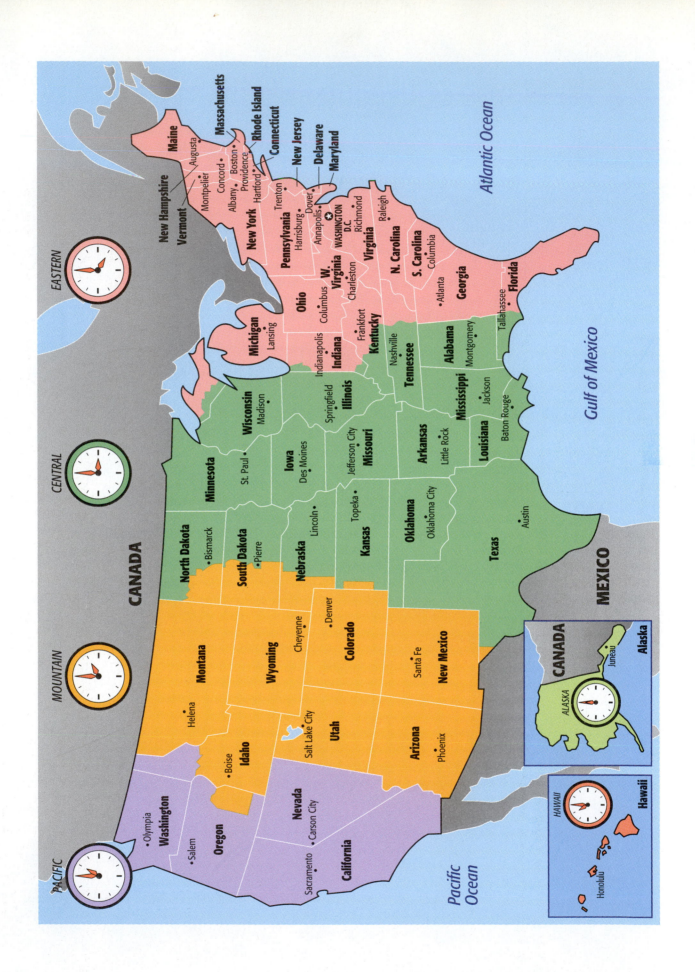

EASTERN

CENTRAL

MOUNTAIN

PACIFIC

CANADA

Atlantic Ocean

Maine
New Hampshire
Vermont
Augusta
Montpelier
Concord
Massachusetts
Boston
Providence
Rhode Island
Connecticut
Albany
Hartford
New Jersey
Trenton
Delaware
Dover
Maryland
Annapolis
WASHINGTON D.C.
Richmond
Raleigh
Virginia
N. Carolina
Columbia
S. Carolina
Atlanta
Georgia
Tallahassee
Florida

New York
Pennsylvania
Harrisburg
W. Virginia
Charleston
Ohio
Columbus
Frankfort
Kentucky
Nashville
Tennessee
Alabama
Montgomery

Michigan
Lansing
Indianapolis
Indiana

Wisconsin
Madison
Springfield
Illinois
Mississippi
Jackson
Baton Rouge
Louisiana

Minnesota
St. Paul
Iowa
Des Moines
Jefferson City
Missouri
Arkansas
Little Rock

North Dakota
Bismarck
South Dakota
Pierre
Nebraska
Lincoln
Topeka
Kansas
Oklahoma
Oklahoma City
Austin
Texas

Montana
Helena
Wyoming
Cheyenne
Denver
Colorado
Santa Fe
New Mexico

Idaho
Boise
Salt Lake City
Utah
Arizona
Phoenix

Washington
Olympia
Oregon
Salem
Nevada
Carson City
Sacramento
California

Gulf of Mexico

MEXICO

CANADA
ALASKA
Juneau
Alaska

HAWAII
Honolulu
Hawaii

Pacific Ocean